Praise for Patti
Become Your Own Matchmaker

"Finally, a book that's optimistic, practical, specific, and really gives you useful advice on how to go out there and meet your man. Patti never condescends, never blames the single girl, but just lets you in on all her hard-earned matchmaking secrets. If you can't afford to hire a matchmaker, this is the next best thing!"

—Liz Tuccillo, *New York Times* bestselling coauthor of
He's Just Not That Into You and author of *How to Be Single*

"A fun and informative read. Patti turns the challenges of dating into a few easy steps that will change your life and get you on the path to finding your soul mate!"

—Oxygen TV stars Tori Spelling, *New York Times*
bestselling author of *sTori Telling* and *Mommywood*,
and her husband, Dean McDermott

"This book is a practical guide to mating in America! Patti Stanger teaches women how to love themselves as women and then give men the opportunity to love themselves by growing into gentlemen."

—Dr. Patricia Allen, coauthor of *Getting to "I Do"*

This title is available from Simon & Schuster Audio and as an ebook.

BECOME YOUR OWN MATCHMAKER

8 EASY STEPS FOR ATTRACTING YOUR PERFECT MATE

Patti Stanger

with Lisa Johnson Mandell

ATRIA PAPERBACK

New York   London   Toronto   Sydney

I dedicate this book to single women everywhere.
If you take one thing away from my book, know this:
If you want him he's out there.

ATRIA PAPERBACK
A Division of Simon & Schuster, Inc.
1230 Avenue of the Americas
New York, NY 10020

First Atria Paperback edition December 2009

ATRIA PAPERBACK and colophon are
trademarks of Simon & Schuster, Inc.

For information about special discounts for bulk purchases,
please contact Simon & Schuster Special Sales at
1-866-506-1949 or business@simonandschuster.com.

The Simon & Schuster Speakers Bureau can bring authors to your
live event. For more information or to book an event, contact the
Simon & Schuster Speakers Bureau at 1-866-248-3049
or visit our website at www.simonspeakers.com.

Designed by Rhea Braunstein

Manufactured in the United States of America

20 19 18 17 16 15 14 13

The Library of Congress has cataloged the hardcover edition as follows:

Stanger, Patti.
   Become your own matchmaker : 8 easy steps for attracting your
perfect mate / by Patti Stanger with Lisa Johnson Mandell.
        p.   cm.
1. Man-woman relationships.   2. Love.   I. Mandell, Lisa Johnson.
II. Title.

HQ801.S759   2009
646.7'7—dc22   2008037963

ISBN: 978-1-4165-5994-8
ISBN: 978-1-4165-9771-1 (pbk)
ISBN: 978-1-4165-9774-2 (ebook)

Contents

Preface

I never took the marriage vow "Till death do us part" too literally. What I feel it really means is "Till there is no more growth of the two souls together, we must part." Well, you don't have to be married to experience this. I, myself, have recently broken up with my fiancé, Andy. I'm sure I will be judged by some as a matchmaker who can't find a match, but those who know me would say I did the right thing. As great a guy as he is, Andy and I were really meant to be friends, not lovers. And I will always treasure my relationship with him as one of the best of my life.

As I grew and evolved I realized the things that I enjoyed he wasn't interested in. As he was ready to retire, I was ready to build my empire. My decision to break things off was probably one of the hardest I've ever had to make. But there's one thing I know for sure, if it feels wrong, don't do it.

I believe that no matter where you are in the world, your true life mate is just waiting to rendezvous with you at a moment's notice, as long as your vibration is in alignment with your desire. You've just got to believe . . . and a belief is nothing more than a thought you think over and over again. Just as a female animal in the wild signals her male to come a-calling, so do humans. I'm not disillusioned by the fact that I'm single now . . . because I believe. Sure, there are dark days here and there—birthdays, holidays, family functions. The hardest times for me are the Saturday nights that I don't have anybody to spend with . . . but thank god for Panasonic. And these times only make me stronger.

I'm in the first chapter of my book "Dating Detox" right now as I write this—something you'll learn all about. It's been so helpful: I'm re-finding things I am passionate about and re-learning all the things I want to do in life. I started making out lists of everything I love and how I want to conquer them. This has helped me tremendously through lonely times:

- COOKING—I love to cook and am a real foodie. I am writing a cookbook because I want to share my passion for food and amazing family recipes with the world.
- LOSING WEIGHT AND WORKING OUT—I have lost 25 pounds and I am working out daily. My blood is pumping and I look and feel better than I ever have before, plus my libido is singing!
- TRAVELING—I couldn't always go to the places I wanted to with Andy because we had to mutually agree on the destination—now I can go anywhere, anytime! Greece and St. Barts, here I come!
- MOVIES—My escape. I am writing a heartfelt romantic comedy with Destin Pfaff that you girls are going to love!

PREFACE

- TV—My other escape. I know it sounds silly, but now I get to watch all the television programs I want to, such as *True Blood* . . . which he wasn't into, or the *Sex and the City* repeats he hated.

Just thinking about these things makes me feel excited! And yes, I still like to spend time visualizing the man I will end up with. The best part of my day is when I'm sitting in my Jacuzzi, candles blazing, listening to my favorite song, "I'll Always Love You," by Taylor Dayne (who happens to be my friend) all while imagining her singing it to my husband and me as we dance at our wedding—a sexy, tall, athletic, independent, wealth builder who has my back . . . and, if I'm lucky, will already have children I can spoil and send to college.

Speaking of children . . . yes, Andy and I did agree to have children when we met, but he changed his mind. It was unfortunate, but, remember, love is a risk and there are no guarantees, even when you stake claim to the Five Non-Negotiables you set (more on this on page 143). Every man and woman has the right to change their mind at any time.

In the end, it's all about taking your time and enjoying the journey without worrying about the destination. I'm looking forward to buying my first house, I'm looking forward to decorating it, and I'm looking forward to the future. And that's something I can do on my own.

As you follow the upcoming eight steps, realize, as I have, that the most important thing during all of this is to be true to yourself. Be authentic and don't settle for a guy who's not everything you want. Look at the important things, disregard the unimportant ones, and be IN LOVE—don't just LOVE him.

Please understand that if you haven't met the person you want by the end of these lessons, it just means that you're on the road to meeting him. There are always signs of land: men asking you out, being in a relationship, or being proposed to. Eventually, you will get your training wheels on and learn to be a man-catcher—the RIGHT man catcher. These steps will get us where we need to be for love. If I had a dollar for every girl who came into my business, The Millionaire's Club, to be coached, then met her husband when she wasn't looking (but was enjoying the process of dating and not taking it too seriously) I would be rich—Oprah rich.

Oh, and one last thing . . . when you do meet him (and you will), and everything works out, pay your knowledge forward. Tell every person—girl, guy, straight, gay, whatever—how to do it. Everyone needs a little help and direction once in awhile—and when it comes to love, not everyone knows the facts, the game plan, or the strategy. Share your expertise and let's get everyone into a relationship . . . the RIGHT relationship!

So girls, I am in the trenches with you now. I know my honey is just about to enter my life . . . and your honey is just about to enter yours!

Love,
Patti . . . xoxo

Introduction

One good orgasm spoils the bunch.

Every time a heterosexual female sleeps with a man—a good one, a bad one, it doesn't matter—she becomes bonded to that man, and no other man can exist for her. This is because the hormone oxytocin starts surging through her veins. So proceed with caution—one good orgasm, and your bonds to any Joe Schmo are chemically reinforced. The more sex you have, the stronger the bond. This is the reason why women all over the world just can't seem to leave their loser boyfriends, even though their brain, friends, family, even the garbage man, are telling them to dump him.

We've all been there. I know I have. So if you're asking yourself, Why should I listen to Patti Stanger about dating and mating? Who the hell is she? Well, let me tell you who I am: I am you. I'm the girl who has been dating for twenty-five years, searching for the one. I was the one crying to God, "Where the hell is he?" But I didn't just stumble around whining. I got down to business and made it my life's work to find the answers to these questions, for myself and for you. I am a third-generation matchmaker and the owner of the most exclusive matchmaking service in the world, The Millionaire's Club. I have seventeen years in the professional dating-service industry. So you see, I made a point of knowing a thing or two about men. And like everybody else, I've got my own personal story to share, so let's start at the beginning.

I, Patti Stanger, was born to be married to a prince. The only problem was, he didn't show up when he was supposed to—probably because I had a major self-image problem that prevented me from attracting him right away. You see, I was adopted, and although I loved my adoptive parents, I always wondered why my biological parents gave me up. Like many adoptees, I subconsciously felt unloved and unlovable.

However, my mother always taught me to be proud of the fact that I was adopted, so I was. I went into show-and-tell during kindergarten at P.S. 193 and told everyone that not only was I adopted, but that I was better than them because I had the privilege of picking my parents, while they were stuck with theirs. Boy, did I upstage Dan Spillman's new puppy! The class went into an uproar and my mother received a call from the teacher telling her that my behavior was highly inappropriate for a five-year-old.

My mother, knowing me well, defended me (as she does to this day). She's a bit of a softie. My outspoken, tough-love approach is probably in my DNA and comes from nature, not nurture. As the story goes, I was nicknamed The Mouth by my grandfather because I spoke in complete sentences by the age of two. I was very independent, and when my mother tried to feed me, I would say in my best Yiddish accent (imitating my grandparents), "Put it down der." So if you think I'm too abrupt for you, I'm sorry, but that's just the way I am. Singles' Boot Camp is now in session, and I'm your drill sergeant.

My mom, Rhoda Goldstein, was the hottest, hippest, sexiest woman in New Jersey: think Dinah Shore meets the King Sisters. She was a tan, icy blonde with a killer body who could get any man from ten paces away. She had what we often refer to as the S factor. She made men sizzle. I, on the other hand, couldn't even make them sputter. The program running through my brain said, "I'm not good enough for a boy to like me," and I never believed it when one did. But to this day my seventy-something-year-old mother can walk the aisles of Publix supermarket in Aventura, Florida, and get men to ask her for her phone number.

But back to the story: before I came along in the '60s, my mom, in her early twenties, was dying to get married (little did she know she would eventually get married three times and the last one, my stepfather Mel, would be the keeper). She hated college and refused to wait for her Ivy League boyfriend to graduate from the University of Pennsylvania. She left college to come home and concentrate on finding her husband, and that's precisely what she did.

Her mother, my grandmother, introduced her to her first husband, Ira. My grandmother had been married to one man all of her life—the most wonderful man in the world, according to everyone. My grandmother was on a mission to find the same thing for her daughter. Both my mother and my grandmother were the token fix-up queens in the neighborhood.

They'd often see a single girl pining away for true love, and before you could say "engagement," they would introduce her to her future husband. They never did it for money; it was enough to hear the local rabbi say "good job" or perhaps to get a chicken or two in exchange for the mitzvah.

The day my mother met her first husband, she already knew how to get her man. He was a tall, handsome Richard Gere look-alike from Brooklyn. He had just moved to New Jersey and didn't know a soul there. He felt like a fish out of water and he needed to get connected to the community, and my family was connected . . . big time. He saw my mother as a way to get him what he needed. Ira was hot and handsome, and the minute he told my mother, "You'll never have to work when you're with me, kid," they were under the chuppah.

They quickly slipped into a suburban lifestyle and tried to get my mother pregnant. After trying every option available to them to no avail, they decided on adoption. Ira would go out drinking with the boys on a regular basis, as most men of that time did, but when I came along, my mother demanded that he stop carousing. He refused. One night she found out that he wasn't just drinking with the boys—he was sleeping with the other chickadees in town. Ira was a textbook skirt chaser. Divorce was not common at the time, but my mother was a strong-willed woman; she kicked him to the curb and went off to find her next husband.

Phil Stanger was your classic garmento: forty years old, five-foot-seven, smoked a cigar, wore custom-made shirts and suits with his initials on the sleeve, smelled of expensive aftershave, wore a gold pinky ring and had a strong Napoleon complex. He had taken care of his family since he was six years old by working at sweatshops in Brooklyn and was a bachelor who had never been married.

He couldn't care less about kids, which was not good news for me. But he wanted my mother bad. She met him while on a terrible blind date on a cruise around New York Harbor. When she decided to go to the bathroom, Phil was standing at the bathroom door, probably trying to pick up women. He noticed her, and not missing a beat, he said, "I'm gonna marry you." My mother rushed into the bathroom, appalled. "I mean, come on, can't you come up with a better line than that?" she asked him as she came out of the bathroom. And so they bantered about it.

What she didn't realize was that he was serious. He simply knew from the moment he saw her that she was his dream girl. It was a classic case, I would learn later, of a man seeing the prototype of everything on his wish list coming together right before his eyes.

Within three months this flashy bachelor had swept my mother off her feet, promised her a lavish lifestyle, and said he wanted to adopt me. So the rumor goes he went to pay $10,000 for me to my first adoptive father, mom's ex, Ira. We moved to a trendy part of New York, which seemed perfect, because my mother had a passion for fashion like no other, and my dad was in the garment trade. But after about ten years of living in New York, my mom grew homesick for Jersey, and we moved to the most elite suburb on the eastern seaboard: Short Hills (think the Beverly Hills of the East Coast).

From the moment I stepped off the bus I knew I was in the wrong place. I was dressed in true fashionista style with my Fred Braun platform shoes and my bell-bottom jeans, only to find the staples of everyone's wardrobe were oxford cloth shirts from Ralph Lauren, corduroy jeans, and Puma sneakers. Everyone was blond, and to make matters worse, so were my mother and my sister (who was also adopted). I clearly was the Cher in a sea of Christie Brinkleys.

Short Hills was Stepford on steroids. All the husbands took the train to New York while their wives spent their days at the beauty salons and country clubs and eating lavish lunches. I loathed every single minute of it. Even though my parents built the most amazing custom house with his and hers bathrooms and closets, I was dying to get out. I simply refused to become a Lady Who Lunched. My dream was to become Sherry Lansing, who was one of the top women in the film industry and the president of Paramount Pictures at the time. I was dying to get to LA any way I could. I lost myself in films on a daily basis and could not stand the shallowness of the neighborhood.

I was sinking fast, and apparently, so was my new dad. At first he was making a ton of money, sending me away to expensive summer camps and taking the family on lavish vacations and expensive shopping sprees. Then the financial troubles set in. No longer being able to keep up with the Joneses, we were ostracized by local society and my parents lost a lot of friends. My dad was obsessed with what people thought. He was the operations manager of his business and sold his share of the company to his partner simply because he wasn't getting the accolades in *Women's Wear Daily* he felt he deserved. That fatal mistake cost the family our future, and I learned some supreme lessons about narcissism, finances, and men.

Every Monday I watched my mother wait for her allowance to pay the bills, and that lump sum of cash was getting smaller and smaller. I swore to myself, like Scarlett O'Hara did, that I would never, ever be poor again, nor would I ever be financially dependent on a man.

While my dad sat on his ass, drinking away the family savings, my mom was a trouper, trying to save what was left of the family. She taught me the art of the sale by going to the garment district, buying things wholesale, and reselling them at a marked-up price back in Jersey. She sold anything she could get her hands on, from classic Cartier Tank watches to Carlos Falchi purses, so that my sister and I would have clothes on our backs. No one was a better salesperson than my mom, as she taught me the art of the "takeaway." I learned that this could be the best negotiating tool a woman could use in her dating life when trying to close a deal with a man. You'll find out more about that later.

My mom tried to teach me that men should chase me. The problem was, my mom grew up in the '50s and '60s, when men married for sex and women married for security— that wasn't happening in the '70s. I read every trashy romance novel from *The Other Side of Midnight* to *Once Is Not Enough*, and waited patiently for my hot husband to show up and make the earth move. But in the '70s and '80s, boys stopped asking girls out. My mom would have her high school boyfriend, Eddie Goldberg, pick her up and give her a corsage, take her to the dance, and bring her home by a respectable eleven o'clock. But the boys in my school would ask my friends and me out by saying, "Hey, wanna go behind the school to Buzz Creek and get high?"

As time went on, it got worse. I'd ask my mother, "Where are all the men? I'm tired of boys." My mother, being the ultimate social butterfly, would encourage me to go to parties and events. Bar Mitzvah season was huge in my neighborhood, but I had a thing for non-Jews. So off I went to my first Christ Church dance with my best friend, Sally. It was the worst dance, yet it had the cutest boys. All the boys were on one side, and the girls were on the other—nobody was connecting. I thought to myself, "This is ridiculous." My friend Sally kept staring at this boy named Michael. As he stared back, I knew they wanted to meet each other. So I boldly walked over and told him that I had the perfect girl for him and introduced him to Sally. They danced the night away. With that, my first successful match, a matchmaker was born. I realized that being a matchmaker could offer me the greatest highs in life. But it put me in an awkward position. As a matchmaker, I was setting up dates for other people, but it was tough to try and attract dates for myself without scaring men off. Good old Mom noticed this and stepped in.

My mom introduced me to my first legitimate boyfriend. His name was Kevin, and he was exactly what the love doctor had ordered. Since the boys in my school were certainly not asking out the girls, I had to go to the next town over: Springfield, New Jersey. Kevin (my first Virgo) was a tall, handsome,

Jewish, Keanu Reeves type: cool enough to hang with the cool kids (the jocks in my school) and smart enough to hang out with the alternative types (the freaks in my school). He was the slow and steady type, taught me how to drive, and also how to get stoned. My parents and his parents were friends, and it seemed to be a match made in heaven.

That was, until one day when I wanted to lose my virginity to him, and he got scared. Okay, so I didn't pick the fastest racehorse at the track, but the sexual tension was killing me. Kevin would teach me another important lesson: let the man lead, even if he goes slow. He gave me the spiel "I just want to be a senior this year, and be free." Even though I followed the advice of my wise grandmother who used to tell me, "Get off the phone after fifteen minutes or you'll have nothing else to talk about when you see each other!" he grew bored of me. Me, a double Gemini with moon in Sag, he grew bored of *me*. I was horrified—he wouldn't even answer my phone calls to give me an explanation. This is why the members of my club, both male and female, always get feedback on their dates. Years later my stoner first love would go off to college, take the standard graduation present of a European backpacking trip, get sidetracked in the Middle East, and become an Orthodox rabbi in Israel. Clearly he was not my soul mate.

What is a soul mate? I wondered. Do we get only one? In the Jewish religion, we're taught that we have a *bashaert*, which, in essence, is your "meant to be." The belief is that we come into this world and God brings us together with our other half. But realistically there are not enough men for all of the women in the world. How do you find your soul mate?

Does he just show up at your doorstep one day when you're ready? Is it like in the movies when the music starts playing and you get all dizzy? Or is he your best friend and you just don't know he's your true love yet? In order to understand all of these elements, I felt I needed to delve into metaphysics, as I wasn't getting the answers I needed from the traditional role models and religion in my life. So I started studying comparative religions and decided that nobody has all the answers. The only thing that made sense to me was astrology, and so I started studying it intensely. I even practiced it professionally for a while, as the director of marketing for the Kenny Kingston Psychic Network. I learned that we only use 10 percent of our brain (if we're lucky), and that there is a subconscious part of ourselves that we are not aware of but that is preprogrammed to attract our mates.

I'm getting off track though; now back to the dog pile of my romantic history. The moment of truth finally arrived: I lost my virginity and the cherry was popped. Only the cherry was not that sweet. I loved the alternative-rocker, long blond-hair type from the wrong side of the tracks, and had a date with rocker Rob, but I had a family function to attend an hour before the date. I was trying to make my ten-minute appearance and get out of there when my mother grabbed me and said, "I have the perfect guy for you!" As "Popsicle Toes" by Michael Franks started playing over the speakers, in walked the most icy-cold, sexy, outspoken lawyer who looked like he wouldn't take no for an answer (I've always been a sucker for a take-charge guy). He kidnapped me, right then and there, for a fabulous night in New York City with his friends. I had the time of my life. Rocker Rob was dust.

Brian was four years older than I was. Our relationship was a bit like a professor teaching a student. Slowly, seductively, he got me to give up my precious jewel on my eighteenth birthday in my maid's room while my parents were out of town. He said with his cold, calculated inflection, "Isn't this great? This is fucking." I, on the other hand, did not feel the earth move like Jacqueline Susann promised, and I was pissed. It was clear that he and I were not a match, but thanks to oxytocin, I was hooked. Yet as the summer wore on, he slowly stopped calling. Again, my heart was broken, and again I went to see the wise shaman, my grandmother. She told me, "Honey, to men, one hole is like any other hole. If you hold out long enough for them to get to know you, that's when they'll fall in love." I was totally confused. After all, I had given him the most precious commodity I could give anyone. How could he just ignore me? Again, nobody seemed to have the answers. Back to the drawing board I went. I was determined to get inside the mind of the bachelor and figure out how he ticked.

Several years later, after I'd graduated from the University of Miami and was working in the garment trade in New York, I met Jake. We worked for the same company but he worked in the Chicago branch, so this was a long-distance relationship, but it was worth the hassle. He had the face of Warren Beatty and the body of Dom DeLuise. He was the funniest guy to ever work at Unionbay jeans, and he was charming, chivalrous, and believe it or not, he was even sexy. However, he was extremely overweight. This was a classic case of liking somebody who is so not your type that you feel like you need to go to the shrink to get your head examined. Remember, chemistry is indefinable. I was warned to stay away from him by my boss—the two of them hated each other. But like a good little defiant child, I had to go there. He was going to be my husband, or so I thought.

One fateful day he called to cancel our Christmas Mexican vacation, *one week before it*, telling me he was instead going off to Rancho La Puerta by himself to lose weight. It was clear he was no longer interested in me. Of course I needed to find out why, so I asked his assistant, my friend Julianne, what happened. "Annabel the aerobics instructor is what happened," she told me. Annabel was a five-foot-two, hundred-pound, yoga-bodied waif who would become Jake's wife. Many months later he told me that if I had just lost fifteen pounds, I would have been a contender. This is when I learned the important lesson that **the penis does the picking**. Now, mind you, I wasn't a professional model but I was often used as the showroom model during times when the flaky professional models didn't show up. I was a classic size 8, which today is considered a 6, and I could fit into sample sizes of our jeans. I had what were considered, in garmento speak, to be fit-model dimensions. I was not fat. But I *was* mad. Why the hell would he date me in the first place if I wasn't the prototype of the woman he wanted? I figured I was sloppy seconds because he couldn't get his first choice. I was determined now more than ever to find out about the beauty/chemistry thing that all men seemed to want. I mean, did you have to be a 10 to attract a marriage-minded man?

The mystery of the marriage-minded man took me to Miami, where I scored a job as the director of marketing at the largest dating service in the country at the time, Great Expectations. I went on a low-carb diet and lost twenty pounds. At five feet eight, 110 pounds on a good day (and 115 when Aunt Flo was in town from Redlands), I got an organic tan, let my hair grow down to my breasts and whitened my teeth. I now felt I had sex-appeal power, and was ready to play on the 10 team. Okay, maybe not 10, but definitely at least 8. With a bright, fresh, outgoing attitude and a great job that took me to all the hot parties, charity events, and galas in town, I was now ready to date like a power player.

Into my life walked a supersexy, tan, Patrick Dempsey type who dressed like he owned Hugo Boss, wore an expensive watch and loafers, and looked like he exemplified money. Matt was the epitome of the Ivy League–educated male who came from a loving, upper-middle-class family that gave him everything. Sadly, the family still paid his bills, Momma worshipped him, and he could not make a dime in life. Although book smart, he was a true lazy slacker who thought the world owed him a living. This type of man would plague me for the rest of my life. Patti loves to pick up the wounded bird in the road and fix it, because she can't fix herself.

But Matt brought something special to the table that no man had ever brought before: he made me feel beautiful and could make me climax repeatedly. I was a goner. I became addicted, obsessed. I was that love junkie who needed her catnip sex. The problem was that Matt wanted me to pay for dates, worship him, and forget I ever had an opinion. We decided to keep the relationship to strictly sex, and I went off to search for my husband, but of course that didn't work either—I was so naïve, and knew nothing about oxytocin bonding. When he got into a serious relationship with another girl and I could not lure him back with my sexual circus tricks, I was so insanely possessed that I went to see a spiritual *santero*, who performed a religious spell to bring him back. Amazingly enough, in twenty-four hours, Sexy came back. The problem is, these spells have an expiration date and can backfire if the sender is not coming from a pure place, and since I wanted control, I was not. The law of Wicca is that anything that you send out will come back to you tenfold—good or bad. My punishment was that for three years I was bonded to a man who was not a good guy—especially not for me. He knew he was using me for sex, he knew he had no interest in a serious relationship with me, and he knew how much he hurt me. Astrologically speaking, his Venus conjuncted my Mars, which is the most powerful aspect in sexual astrology. Knowing this was a consolation prize for me. But because oxytocin bonding can take up to two years to diminish, I was no prize for anyone else.

Three years later I met the man who told me he wanted to marry me on the first date. He was drop-dead gorgeous, a Christian Bale look-alike, six feet two, ripped, and was in the entertainment business. He was my first serious non-Jewish boyfriend. I was madly in love, and all my fears that Matt would be the best sex I'd ever had went away when I met Paul. Paul was the epitome of chivalry and romance. He sent roses every week to my office, with cute love notes that all my coworkers read and envied. He also had a radio voice, deep, sexy, and rugged—all the women in my office wanted to talk to him on the phone when he called. I would later learn that women fall in love between their ears and not with their eyes, simply because we are emotional and need to hear the tone of a man's sincerity before we commit.

But problems soon arose because he was much simpler than I was, and in some ways I guess he felt that I was high maintenance. I never, ever asked for anything financially and was willing to pay my own way in our relationship. But when it came down to actually getting engaged, he told me he didn't ever want to have children, and that was a deal breaker at the time. Later I would learn that qualifying your buyer before having sex is crucial. I should have found out that important little piece of information before I ever slept with him—and bonded with him.

So I continued my romantic quest. After a while I felt I had "done" Miami as it's a small town where everybody knows each other. I moved to Los Angeles to pursue my dream of getting into the film industry. The best advice I ever got was from Arthur Cohn at Paramount who said to me, "You are an idea person who thinks big. You should never work for anybody else . . . start your own business." At first I thought he was giving me a line because he didn't want to give me a job. But the truth was, he was right. I had to take a job to pay the bills, so I got a generic Fortune 500 job in marketing. While working in a boring job I needed excitement at night, so I signed up for all of the dating services I could find and again started the hunt for the husband. This time I will spare you all the bad dates, all the flakes, all the looky-loos I encountered. Coming from the East Coast where you can set your watch to the time a date shows up, I was completely lost in LA, where everyone seems to flake out. I did not know a soul and cried myself to sleep every single night, wondering what the hell was wrong with me.

One day I got a date with a man one of the agencies I'd signed up for set me up with, who complained about that company's lack of customer service. He was wealthy, ready to marry, and just wasn't able to find the right girl. He was socially inept, however. He asked me out only hours before a New Year's Eve party, perfectly ready to cancel his preexisting date. All East Coast girls know that no matter how much you like a guy, you never accept a last-minute date. I told him that I really appreciated the offer, but I already had plans. He pursued me, but I decided I wasn't interested and put him in the Friend Zone. I also told him he needed to redo his wardrobe if he wanted to get laid. That's how the Millionaire's Club began. He invested $10,000 in my fledgling company, got himself a new wardrobe, and bought an expensive leather jacket for me. I soon introduced him to his future wife; they became my first clients to marry and have a baby—a beautiful baby girl. He was so appreciative that he spread the word and clients came calling.

It was expensive to get my business going, but with what little money I had left, I bought a small ad in *Los Angeles* magazine. LA seems to have the largest percentage of single millionaires in the United States who are willing to pay to play. Little did I know that not only would millionaires call me, but so would average Joes. I would go off during the day to do pro bono work making matches in the local community for those who couldn't afford my services, while fixing up my millionaire clients at night. Great Expectations had given me great training for recruiting new members, and I started a dating revolution by offering the service to women for free. I was making bank and quit my Fortune 500 job so I could work from home.

I soon realized there was also a huge market for matching millionairesses as well as gay millionaires. With a hundred and ten million single adults in the United States and growing, singledom was no longer for the dateless and desperate. Everyone was on the Internet, blind dating, joining matchmaking services, and text messaging to find love.

One day I got a call from *Marie Claire* magazine. The editor asked me to help with a story on gold diggers. As much as I love that magazine, I refused. I told the editor I don't have gold diggers in my service; I have women who want to fall in love with rich men. Gold diggers are flippers, like in real estate—they cannot form solid, long-term relationships. My women want the choice of staying home, raising their families, or going off to work if they choose to without the pressure of being the main breadwinner. Rich men afford them that lifestyle. The editor of the magazine was shocked, and I think appalled, but she called me back twenty-four hours later to tell me they would write the story I wanted, about decent women who want to date and marry wealthy men, not gold diggers. And so they did, and many more magazine articles and TV appearances followed. That put me on the map and enabled me to bring you this book.

To answer the question you're doubtlessly asking right now, no, I'm still not married. So why should you take my advice? The truth is, in my forties I realized something about myself—I don't have to be married to be happy. I wish I would have learned that a lot earlier—it would have saved me a lot of heartache. That doesn't mean that I won't get married one day, but for now I'm in a four-and-a-half-year, happy relationship. My boyfriend, who I was introduced to by a matchmaker, is loving, caring, sexy, and fun, and he is my best friend. I wish this type of man for every one of you, so you will know the feelings of unconditional love that I experience daily.

If you are one of the millions of women who wants to find her perfect match and marry him, then this is the book for you. I'll teach you not only how to find the love of your life, but how to negotiate an engagement, complete with ring, in one year. You might have read a lot of dating books, as I have. But it seems every book is missing at least one element that is essential for closing the deal. I promise you this book will tell you, show you, and teach you what you've done wrong and how to do it right. It will clear up all the mysteries that momma could not teach you, but more important, it will empower you to love yourself and clear the path to your perfect match.

At the end of your life, when you're on your deathbed,

you won't be able to take the cars, the house, the money, or any material things with you. All you'll be able to take is the love you've acquired in your lifetime. Romantic, unconditional love is something everyone not only strives for, but needs in order to feel complete. I answer to a higher authority, and as your romantic fairy godmother who gets credits in heaven when she makes a match, may this book bestow you your husband and bring you everlasting love.

STEP ONE

Dating Detox

Recovering from a bad relationship? Been on a series of disaster dates? Are you a one-date wonder? Just got dumped? Haven't been on a date in weeks, months, or years? Maybe you're a serial dater who can't make a relationship last more than two months. If you fall into any of these categories (and what single woman doesn't?) your first step is to go through Dating Detox. During this step you get to stop, take a deep breath, and get your romantic bearings. This is probably my favorite step of all, because it's all about me—excuse me—I mean, it's all about you. It's not about men, not about friends or family, it's not about pleasing anyone else—you purely focus on pleasing yourself.

During this time you wrap yourself in a delicious, warm and cuddly cocoon to metamorphose into the sexy, irresistible femme fatale that's buried deep inside you. **Don't even think about going out on a date.** Just step back and take time to figure out what exactly it is that you're looking for and what makes YOU happy. This is a chance to get back in touch with your softer, more feminine side—to draw men to you like bees to honey.

On a side note, don't be surprised if during your dating sabbatical, the men start lining up. As soon as you say, "I'm not going to date for a while," the bus unloads. Don't go out with them, but make sure you take reservations. Remember, the best restaurants are booked weeks in advance, why not you? You're worth waiting for.

Depending on the length of your last serious relationship, Dating Detox should last between thirty to ninety days. If your most recent relationship lasted less than a year or if you've never had a serious relationship, detox for thirty days. If your last relationship lasted for two years, detox for sixty days. If it was a marriage or a relationship that lasted three or more years, detox for ninety days. Believe me, you'll end up loving Dating Detox so much you might need someone close to you to slap you and make you move on from it.

The Happiest Place on Earth

One of the reasons this step is so delectable is that for thirty to ninety days, you're allowed to completely forget your troubles. Once you get the positive energy flowing, you'll move into a place of happiness that you'll never want to leave. This happiness will be unflappable—you'll be able to be happy anytime, anywhere, even with the most obnoxious people around you or, even more important, alone. As soon as you learn to revel in the opportunity to be by yourself rather than languish in miserable isolation, you'll be free of that ugly and burdensome feeling known as desperation. And once you've attained internal happiness, you'll be ready for a mature, solid relationship. A happy woman makes a much better companion, and your stock on the dating market will soar.

Men love happy women. It's as simple as that. Hell, women, children, dogs, cats—everyone loves, and wants to be with, a happy woman. The happier you are, the happier your mate will be. The truth behind the law of attraction is that like attracts like. During my matchmaking events I often see cheerful women who are not classically beautiful attracting more men than the supermodels in the room. Why? Because the supermodels are more likely to be starving and insecure, and don't exactly exude joie de vivre.

Are you that happy person? If not, ask yourself why. Many clients come to me unhappy because they don't have a man. I tell each one that her attitude will only set her back because a man will only be drawn to her once she realizes that she can be happy without him. Men see women who are with them because they *choose* to be, not because they *need* to be. Most women don't understand this. They think they're losers because they don't have Saturday night dates, but this couldn't be further from the truth. It's far better to wait for the right guy, alone in your jammies, than to be out with someone you have no interest in, wasting time and money.

Another common reason you might be unhappy is because you're weighed down by issues from your past. We all have issues. Even the happiest, most well-adjusted woman you know has had her share of problems, I can assure you. As I mentioned before, I had to overcome the issues I had with being adopted. Now is the time to tackle your demons head-on and get over them. There's a great line in the brilliant, semiautobiographical Carrie Fisher movie, *Postcards from the Edge*, where Lowell says, "I don't know your mother, but I'll tell you something. She did it to you and her mother did it to her and back and back and back all the way to Eve and at some point you just say, 'Fuck it, I start with me.'"

Release your past and say, "Today's the day I start with me!" Why would you want to drag all the problems you've already hashed and rehashed, ad nauseam, into a new relationship? Bite the bullet and get therapy, if you think you need it. A word about therapy: I've worked extensively with therapists and psychiatrists in my business, but I would suggest choosing your therapist very carefully and finding one that's truly right for you. And if you've been seeing the same therapist for years and don't feel like you've made much progress, perhaps it's time to move on. Like a professional athlete—if you want to win Wimbledon, you need the right coach to get you there.

Bitter Women Beware

The vast majority of women in Dating Detox are going to have some unresolved man issues. We've all had them. But now is the time to say, "I forgive all the men who came before; I start with me!" Forgiveness lightens your load. One of the most important keys to dating success lies in not becoming The Bitter Woman. Men can smell this type from a mile out and will run in the opposite direction. During Dating

Detox you need to learn to love and trust the opposite sex. You need to stop complaining about men and focus on their redeeming qualities. Most important, you must accept the fact that you're never going to change them.

Jenna is a perfect example of a woman mired in bitterness. She's about twenty pounds overweight and refuses to exercise or change her eating habits. "Most men are pigs, because they only focus on the physical. I'm looking for an enlightened guy who will love me for me and doesn't care about what kind of shape I'm in. Until I find him, the rest can all go to hell," she says. Guess what? She's never going to find him. He doesn't exist. And even if he did, he would be thrown off by her me-against-the-world attitude. If Jenna ever wants to get married, and she claims she does, she not only needs to lose the weight (for her own health's sake, at least), she needs to lose the attitude.

During Dating Detox, you stop dwelling on all the Bad Boyfriends of the past, and you look forward to all the wonderful experiences you're going to have with men in the future. Take heart in knowing that most happily married women will gladly tell you it was worth going through every bad breakup, every creepy ex, every unbearable date, to finally find their True Love. Think of yourself as a great wine—you're only getting better and more valuable with age. When the right occasion comes along and that wine is uncorked, it will be the best, most delicious nectar the lucky partaker has ever experienced. But that will only happen if happiness is a major ingredient.

I know it isn't easy to just wake up one morning and

decide, "Okay, enough dwelling on the past. I'm now going to be a happy person!" The sad truth is that most women spend so much time trying to please others—their families, their coworkers, their neighbors, their friends, their romantic partners—that they don't even know what it takes to please themselves. When I ask you, "What makes you happy?" can you immediately list ten things that make you smile, or do you have to stop and think about it for a few minutes . . . hours . . . days?

The Quick, Happy Fix

If you're among those stumped (and I know I was, for many years), I want you to sit down during Dating Detox and make a list of the things that make YOU happy. Not the things that your mother would like to see on the list. Not the things that the Bible tells you to enjoy. Your list doesn't have to include grand accomplishments, like getting a PhD, living in a mansion, winning the lottery, or having twins. Let's take baby steps, and start thinking about life's simple pleasures. Here are a dozen quick happiness fixes for you to consider:

1. Get lost in your favorite book, TV show, or movie. Rent *Gone with the Wind*. Indulge yourself in your favorite chick lit. Have a *Sex and the City* marathon.
2. Take a long hot bath with your favorite scented bath oil or bubbles—candles and soft music are nice as well.
3. Take a quick weekend vacation. Was there a place you

used to love as a child? If not, a spa weekend is always fun. If you're on a budget, get some girls together and go camping. Or maybe go visit your favorite cousin whom you haven't seen in ages.

4. Pet, hold, or hug something soft and furry, even if it's just at the pet store. You could also offer to walk your neighbor's dog.

5. Work on your favorite hobby. Even if you haven't enjoyed it since high school, get back to painting, photography, scrapbooking, knitting, training for a triathlon, baking the best chocolate chip oatmeal cookies on the planet, or whatever it is you do that allows you to express your creativity and makes you feel a sense of accomplishment.

6. Write a nice letter. Email doesn't count. Take pen in hand and write to someone you care for and tell them how much you appreciate them.

7. Plant something. Have you always wanted an herb garden or pretty flowers by your door? Gardening is both relaxing and rewarding.

8. Listen to happy music. Forget the whiny girl stuff, the violent, misogynistic rap, and the songs that make you long for lost loves. I love you, Alanis Morissette, but you have to go. I don't care if you have to download a collection of your favorite TV theme songs, just listen to something that makes you want to move and feel good.

9. Sign up for a class or workshop. Ever wanted to make

sushi? Learn more about wine? Master sensual massage? Now's the time!

10. Explore your roots. Find out who you are, where you came from. You can google the word "genealogy" and you'll instantly come up with dozens of sites that will help you learn about your ancestors. You can also make calls to members of your family who might have already climbed your family tree. Gaining a sense of who you are and where you came from is a wonderful thing.

11. Eat chocolate. I have some reservations about recommending this because once you start, it's so hard to stop and you certainly don't want to overindulge, but a piece of rich, dark chocolate can be good for both your heart and soul. Teuscher Champagne Truffles are my personal favorites—make sure your vibrator is nearby.

When Purging Is Good

Since you're not worrying about finding and dating men, either online or in person, you'll also have plenty of time to rid your life and your surroundings of all the things that DON'T make you happy. Clean house. Purge. It might be painful, but this is the ideal time to get rid of all those pictures of ex-boyfriends and those silly little gifts they gave you. It's especially important to get rid of anything that carries his scent, like a T-shirt or sweatshirt. We're chemically drawn to our partner's natural scent, which is why we like to smell his shirt when he's not around—remember *Brokeback Mountain?* You'll never get over him if you don't dispose of everything that smells like him. Now, if the expensive gifts he's given you are too valuable to toss out, pass them along to a friend or sell them.

The real principle behind cleaning house has nothing to do with removing all traces of the ex so you won't get all misty eyed every time you see them or so the new boyfriend won't find them. It's far deeper than that. You're making room for new things to come into your life. Suze Orman encourages women to clean out their purses and wallets to get rid of the old junk so there will be plenty of space for new money to come in. Try it. Create a vacuum, and the universe will fill it. You'll be amazed at how well this works. If you sell that Cartier watch, there will be room on your wrist for a Patek Philippe from your next boyfriend and you can use the extra cash to buy a few pairs of Jimmy Choos—to (symbolically) walk on your ex.

Happy + Active = Attractive

Ever wonder why, when you're all sweaty, out of breath, and looking your absolute worst after a heavy workout, some guy picks that precise moment to hit on you? You think, "Dude, if you like me now, you should see me when I'm wearing makeup and a skirt!"

Believe it or not, after a workout you are at your most attractive to men, because you're all glowy from that endorphin rush; you're calm, happy, content, and for a few minutes or hours, you are not thinking about dating. My clients tell me they can't resist a woman who is centered on something other than finding a man, and is instead focused on something that makes her happy and vibrant. This is why I encourage all the girls in my club to exercise—of course, this also offers them the opportunity to firm up and lose weight.

So, during Dating Detox you'll definitely want to find an exercise regimen that makes you happy. If you're a Zen type, yoga and meditation will do it for you. If you're a Type A personality like I am, you won't have the patience for yoga, and you'll want to do something more active. The workout I've found that works best for me is exercising on an elliptical machine while watching a romantic tearjerker or catching up on all the TV shows I've recorded and haven't had time to watch. My writing partner, Lisa, is on what she calls the "Netflix diet." She rents a movie from Netflix and won't allow herself to see any of it unless she's on the elliptical machine, working up a sweat. The better the movie, the longer and more frequently she works out.

Please Please Me

Once you've discovered how to please yourself, it's time to start thinking about how others can please you, in particular, your soul mate. Remember, don't think of him as the prize for which you're competing against hundreds of other women. YOU are the prize, and HE needs to please you just as much as you need to please him. So what type of man will it take to win your affection and devotion? What is your type? What do you value in a partner? I have a method of discovering this that is really fun and happens to involve the only date you get to have during Dating Detox—a date with yourself.

Don't be disappointed—no one knows you better, is more supportive, or wants you to succeed more than your own sweet self. And besides, this is the part where you get to really treat yourself. Go to your favorite market or restaurant and order the food you love most. (Incidentally, the food you love most will not be bad for you or make you fat, right?) Me? I'd go to the Whole Foods food bar, rush past the crème brûlée French toast (even though I love it), and load up on all my organic, free-range favorites—chicken, salad, etc. If you're a wine drinker, get a bottle of your favorite, and promise yourself that you'll drink just one glass with dinner and maybe half a glass during this next exercise.

After you've treated yourself to that delicious meal, get comfortable and relax. Tonight you'll begin to get your mind in sync with what you truly desire. You are going to create a picture of your perfect mate in your mind. After all, how will you ever recognize him if you don't know what he's like?

A fun and provocative way to get started with this is to take fifteen minutes to make a list of your most recent boyfriends, not listing more than five. Write down their top five assets—the things that really attracted you to them in the first place and made you stay with them as long as you did. Then list their five worst traits—the things that drove you crazy, that made you break up with them, or want to punch them, or kill them, or both. Don't get bogged down on this, though—remember, we're not dwelling on the past, and we're not dwelling on the negative. Fifteen minutes should be plenty for this part of the exercise.

Now, I don't care if you're eighteen or eighty, there must be someone you've met along the way with whom you really would have liked to have had a relationship, if the circumstances had been right. Do you admire a friend's husband or boyfriend? List five reasons you'd like to be with a guy like that, and five reasons why you wouldn't. Or if the men around you are particularly uninspiring, tap Hollywood. God knows I go there in my mind every now and then for inspiration. My apologies to my wonderful boyfriend, but I've used Viggo Mortensen more than once for a number of different types of inspiration.

Winners and Losers List

I'll tell you what to do with your lists soon, but before I do, let me share a story to keep you motivated. Lisa, my writing partner, was one of those people who used to be attracted to anything new or different with a penis. She was all over the map with the men she dated, hoping that she would one day stumble upon her "type." Only problem was, she didn't have a clue what her type was. When she finally decided it was time to settle down into a serious relationship, I advised her to make this list and analyze it. Now, I don't mean to sound like a miracle worker . . . okay, maybe I do. But *two months* after Lisa made her list, she met the man of her dreams, to whom she is now blissfully married. She knew by the fifth date that he was the one for her, and he knew even sooner. I know, I know, it makes you a little sick at first, but if you saw her list of ex-boyfriends, you wouldn't envy her so much. It was right after the intolerant evangelical, whom Lisa refers to as the Last Bad Boyfriend, that she finally decided to take my advice and go into Dating Detox. After all, her relationship experience was not helping her make better choices; in fact, her choices were getting progressively worse. Lisa desperately needed to take some time off from men to decide what she was really looking for so that she would attract that. She was suffering from what I call Shiny Ball Syndrome—going after any shiny object that came along without even considering what it would take to make her truly happy in the long run.

But enough about Lisa. Let's take a look at your list. I'm most interested in the strengths category. Are there certain traits that appear more than once? Those are probably the attributes that mean the most to you. It's interesting to note that the younger you are, the more physical traits will be on you strengths list. The older you are, you'll probably be more attracted to character traits. The over-forty crowd can usually see a pattern and decide what they want in a man pretty quickly—after all, we've had a lot more experience with different types of men. But if you're under forty, it might take a little more time to really decide what's important to you. The next section will help you out.

Living in Five Different Worlds

Don't worry if you're a little confused about what you really want in a mate. I've known brilliant women with master's degrees and PhDs from the best schools, who were clueless about what's most important to them. In fact, it's usually the smartest ones who take the longest to get married, because they can't get their minds in sync with their hearts and bodies. They lean too heavily on the intellectual, at the expense of just about everything else. We all live in five distinct worlds: Spiritual, Physical, Emotional, Intellectual, and Financial. Of course, none of us divide our time equally between them. Think about which worlds are most important to you. Now think about how important it is for your ideal mate to match up to your preferences in each of these categories. If this sounds complicated, let me give you a little help.

SPIRITUAL: You don't have to be religious to be spiritual— this just means that you have a connection with someone or something beyond the physical world. I consider myself a spiritual person. I was raised in the Jewish faith, but I consider myself more of a Food Jew—when the food shows up, I show up. I'm observant on significant holidays, because I like to spend them with those I love. But I'm very metaphysical. I don't belong to any particular organized congregation. I believe that organized religion is manufactured by man, not God. But I do believe in the power of the universe. I call on it often, and I do my best to keep in sync with it.

Sounds a little airy-fairy, I know, but it works for me. The point I'm making about spirituality is that yours should mesh with your ideal mate's. You don't need to have the exact same beliefs, but you should respect each other's and honor them. If either one of you feels resentful or derisive of the other's faith, it's not going to be a good match. And he needs to be more than just tolerant of the faith you practice, or the faith you grew up with.

Here's a crazy story about faith for you: I know of a really fabulous woman who escaped from a polygamist compound on the southern Utah/Arizona strip. Although she no longer believed in The Principle, she was worried that no man in his right mind would ever love a woman with a background like hers. She enrolled in a university, went to grad school, and there she met a man who was not only tolerant of her past, he encouraged her to associate with her family and even helped some of her half brothers and sisters start productive lives outside of the compound. He is a truly spiritual person in that he believes in the good of all mankind and works to help his fellow human beings find their true path.

It's also very important that neither one of you feels that you are giving up your religion or sacrificing spirituality for the other. This will only lead to disharmony and frustration in the long run, and when one of you finds someone who is more spiritually compatible, the temptation to stray will be irresistible. Even though your devotion to your beliefs may be unique and may limit your options, if your particular faith is really important to you, I encourage you to stand firm. As my grandmother used to say, there's a lid for every pot. Yours is out there; it just might take you a little longer to find him. Besides, places of worship are great for finding your perfect match.

Beware the hypocrites, however. People are probably more hypocritical about their spirituality than just about any other aspect of their personality. Actually, a lot of my clients are like that. I had a super Zen yoga master who lied, cheated on his wife with his devotees, and yelled at his staff. A man who is hypocritical about his spirituality is going to be dishonest in other areas of his life as well, so be careful. There are men out there who will tell you what they think you want to hear. It's very hip to be "spiritual" right now, but if that's important to you, you need to make sure he walks the walk and talks the talk.

PHYSICAL: We women like to think that what's on the outside doesn't matter as much to us as what's on the inside. Although *we* may give a guy we're not initially attracted to a second date because he has some really great character traits, while a man will accept you or dismiss you in the first five minutes, depending on the "schwing factor." Let's face it, we all have our physical preferences—we all have a certain "type."

If you think you're beyond that, let me ask you this: how would you feel about sleeping with a three-hundred-fifty-pound mound of masculine flubber? One of the girls in my club tried it once. She'd spoken to a particular guy numerous times on the phone and thought he was terrific. He showed up at her door wearing an impeccably tailored suit (and probably a man girdle), and although he did look quite large, she thought she could overlook it—he was just so damn nice and funny. He fell head over heels in love with her in the first five minutes; after all, she was hot—about an 8 on a scale of 1–10. He proposed to her on the fifth date, ring and all. While she gently told him she thought it was a little too soon for an engagement, she decided the time was right to sleep with him and test out their physical chemistry. She knew it was going to be dicey, so while he was in the bathroom, she conjured up visions of Colin Farrell from that excruciatingly sexy video that was circulating on the internet a few years back.

Once she opened her eyes and beheld her date naked, however, that vision popped like an overinflated balloon, and so did their relationship. It was obvious the poor guy had once weighed as much as five hundred pounds, and while he was still making an effort to lose more, he had pouches of baggy skin hanging all over him like big rubber curtains. She said it was bad—I mean on-the-verge-of-vomiting bad. She was able to control her urge to puke and bolt, and instead told him she'd had a little too much champagne and asked him if they could cuddle for a while. After feigning sleep she "woke up" later and went home. So much for mind and heart over matter. She still thought the world of him as a human being, but she simply *could not* go there physically.

My advice is to pick the two physical traits that are the most important to you and focus on those. Anything else is icing on the cake. For me, it's hair and height. He doesn't have to be muscle bound, athletic, or have perfect teeth and long eyelashes, just as long as he has a full head of hair and tops six feet. Again, it might be helpful to conjure up a vision of a movie star you're completely attracted to, and think about the two physical traits that turn you on most. Subtract the rest. For example, wanting a perfect masculine life form like George Clooney is greedy and ridiculous. But how about a George Clooney type with a little pot belly? Surely he would do? Or a Brad Pitt with a receding hairline? You know what I mean. You're not perfect, so you really can't expect perfection in return. I cringe every time I see a woman in my club turn down a wonderful man just because "he has red hair" or "he's not hot enough for me." They obviously don't understand that men who are too handsome are usually vain, spend too much time in the bathroom and gym, depend on their looks at the exclusion of everything else, and have too many other gorgeous women after them. Besides, even if he looks perfect, when he opens his mouth he probably sounds like Pee-wee Herman, or he doesn't have a job, or a car, or . . . well, you get the point.

Still not convinced that that outrageously beautiful man is not for you? Let's get realistic here—if you wait until you find Adonis, you'll still be waiting in the nursing home. As my aunt says, in the beginning what's really important is that "when he kisses you, your toes curl." Of course that palpable lust that makes your pulse rush and your VJ get all warm and mushy will die down eventually. Although it should be there in the beginning, no one can sustain that. Sex with him can't be a Broadway opening every night, so you have to find yourself a good spooner. The überhandsome guy is not a good spooner. He thinks that just being with him should be enough of a thrill for you, so after he's gotten his rocks off, he'll turn over and hug himself. I know this man. So just take my advice and pick your two most important physical traits. If he has beautiful eyes and is in good shape, who cares if he waxes his chest? (Yes, I've had girls complain about that.) If you're five feet two and he's five feet eleven, who cares if he's not over six feet?

EMOTIONAL: What you're really looking for here is the emotional yin to your yang. What you're not looking for is a mate who is on the same emotional page that you are. Do you really want a guy who cries every time he sees *A League of Their Own*? Do you want someone who becomes outraged about the same issues you do? Just imagine if you both couldn't stand bad restaurant service and both started screaming at the waiter? You'll mesh best with someone who can calm you down when you're feeling tense, and will appreciate the same from you. Now *that's* a good match and will come in handy when he can take care of the matters you hate even mentioning. Let's say it's time to lease a new car, and you want to start pulling your hair out just thinking about dealing with the car salespeople. Your partner, on the other hand, absolutely relishes the opportunity to shop around and get a killer deal—it's second only to sex in his book. You two could be made for each other.

Of course, there are many other issues in life that are more important than purchasing a new car. You'll want to pay close attention to how he handles stress, disappointment, victory, embarrassment, sadness, loneliness, joy, and myriad other emotions. He doesn't need to handle them the same way you do, you just have to be okay with the way he does handle them. Does he deal with problems head-on, or does he deny them? When troubled, does he become talkative or aloof? Which do you prefer? How do you want to be treated?

Tenderly, or do you like it a little rough every now and then? Does he listen to you sympathetically, or does he race ahead to what he thinks is the solution? Do you like to be nurtured when you're sick, or do you just want him to go away and leave you alone?

Also, pay attention to how he treats his own family. Make sure he has a decent relationship with at least one family member, and bonus points if he's close to at least one sister. But beware the man who has no close relationships with any relatives. Even if they have drastically divergent standards, values, and morals, if family is important to him, you'll find some common ground. If family is not important to him, what makes you think he'll want to start a family with you?

INTELLECTUAL: I'll tell you right now that I prefer to use degrees of laughter, rather than degrees of education, as a barometer for intellectual compatibility, but others disagree. I think people get overly concerned about the amount of education their mate may or may not have. If he "gets" you and makes you laugh, what more do you need? I mean, we all know someone like Miranda, the redhead lawyer on *Sex and the City*, who was happy marrying Steve the bartender.

I've learned from my clients that a man can be intellectually stimulating even if he hasn't been to college. Michelle, an Ivy League–educated business executive, didn't respect men who were less degreed than she was, and believed they would resent her. Then she met her uneducated actor boyfriend who introduced her to the joys of National Public Radio and Pulitzer Prize–winning author Michael Chabon. How had she gone through her entire, ivory-tower life without being aware of either one? Now, she didn't end up marrying him, but she couldn't deny that her no-degree boyfriend wasn't the dummy she expected him to be.

If you can find at least two intellectually stimulating activities you like to do together, I'd say you're in pretty good shape. Do you love to watch foreign/independent films together? Do you both love wine tasting? Have you done the *New York Times* crossword puzzle on Sunday together? Do you enjoy discussing politics? You don't have to agree necessarily, but it's good if you enjoy the debate—it can even be sexually stimulating. Do you like to go to the same types of museums and exhibits? When you travel, do you both like to explore the culture and do as much sightseeing as possible, or do you both like to just unwind on the beach or in the mountains? Maybe you're both into extreme-sports vacations? Do you like to read the same books, newspapers, or websites? If your favorite news sources are TMZ and Perez Hilton and his favorites are the *Wall Street Journal* and *The NewsHour with Jim Lehrer*, I'm not saying it will never work, but be prepared to endure eternal ribbing (I know I do). Just be aware that street smart can be a good match for book smart, if neither one of you is too invested in your own particular form of higher education.

FINANCIAL: This category might seem crass and material-istic, but money is the root of at least 51 percent of all di-vorces. After all, I *am* the Millionaire Matchmaker, and I've witnessed money make or break a relationship more times than I can count. Whatever your financial desires, you just better make sure that the guy you're dating has the same goals you do. So if you want the high life, you better make sure he does too.

On a side note, it's okay to want a wealthy man. It's okay to want a man who makes more money than you do. What's not okay is to be a gold digger or expect to be rescued. A gold digger is a flipper who isn't looking for a long, solid relation-ship. Once she gets what she wants, she'll leave him and trade up. **Gold diggers like to cash in and cash out—they're only interested in leasing, never buying.** On the other hand, a woman who just wants the comfort and security that comes from a wealthy mate also wants to be a good companion as well as have one, and hopes to add as much to his life as he does to hers. It's completely understandable if you want a wealthy husband so you can stay home and take care of the kids, or, if you're past childbearing age, so that you can travel the world together. Just don't be a gold digger.

That being said, the sense of entitlement I see in so many women these days really rubs me raw. One of the girls in my club, a MAW (model/actress/whatever) once asked me, "He only makes two-hundred-and-fifty thousand dollars a year. Is that enough?"

"Enough for WHAT?" I exploded. "Enough to buy you a big house and car and save you from ever having to spritz perfume in a department store again? How much do you make? Do you think that's enough for him? Let me ask you something: what have you got to offer, other than your good looks, which will fade?" Clearly this woman was a gold digger. A wealthy man wants a woman who will act responsibly with his money and help him increase it, not someone who does nothing more than sit around and think of ways to spend it. That's a bad investment, and men don't get rich by making bad investments. I always say, **"She who asks for everything gets nothing. She who asks for nothing gets the world."**

But while money is an important factor to consider, if you meet a great guy who has everything you want except cash, and you turn him away because he hasn't made it yet, you might regret it until the day you die—he could have been the great love of your life. My mother's friend is the perfect example of this—she was dating a great, energetic, motivated, and ambitious guy. Only problem was, he was from the wrong side of the tracks and didn't have two pennies to rub together. Her parents told her to stop seeing him. "But Mom!" she said. "I love him." "I don't care," her mom responded. "He'll never amount to anything." That was Don Kirshner, who eventually became a wealthy, famous music promoter. Not only did she lose him, but she had to hear about him all the time on the radio and television.

A happier story is Karen's—she met and married Michael when they were sophomores in college. They were both preppy paupers, and they finished school while living in a one-room, windowless basement apartment underneath a pizza parlor. They supported each other through thick and thin, and twenty years later they're living in a 10,000-square-foot grand estate with all the money they will ever need and have six beautiful and intelligent children. The lesson here is that while they both aspired to financial success, neither wrote the other one off because he or she wasn't making the big bucks when they first met. Instead, they shared the same goals and grew their life together. It wasn't like the rich guy picked out the Pretty Woman hooker and brought her up to his level.

If You Build Him . . .

He will come. Now that you know who you're looking for, it's time to bring him into your life. I'm a firm believer in manifestation and have followed the teachings of Esther and Jerry Hicks and Abraham for years. So in order to manifest your dream guy, I have a specific recipe for you to follow:

1. Get happy before you begin your manifestation process. Do whatever it takes to get into this place: eat chocolate, pet your puppy, play golf, take a bath, watch your favorite comedy . . . you get the point. Beware: If you do not complete this critical step, your manifestation will not occur. Others who teach this process leave out this vital step but trust me, your happiness is the fuel that will take you to where you want to go.

2. Close your eyes for a minimum of seventeen seconds, preferably more. Visualize how you want your particular desire to play out. You are the author, the director,

and the actor of the movie in your mind. For example, if you want the cute guy at the gym to ask you out, picture him standing in front of you and asking you out. If you want to go away on vacation with someone you just met, imagine him taking you away to a romantic destination. If you want to get married, imagine yourself walking down the aisle in a beautiful dress. If you don't have a particular person in mind to marry, imagine your favorite celebrity crush to get you closer to the target. The more you visualize how you want your life to be, from a happy place, the quicker it will happen.

3. Now let go of the scene, but come back to it anytime you want and add more details to it.

Continue practicing this exercise with the things you want in your life, and the practice will soon become so much fun and so satisfying that you'll enjoy the visualization itself, without focusing on whether or not it happens. This is important because the universe will only reward you when you are in a place of desiring without keeping score.

Half the fun is in the anticipation of your perfect mate. You will find yourself so deliciously caught up in enjoying the idea of him that before you know it, he'll be tapping you on the shoulder. You'll be more than ready for him. You'll turn around, look him in the eye, smile, and just *know*. And wonder of wonders, so will he!

While you're waiting for your larger desires to arrive, here's a fun little exercise to try that I guarantee won't take very long to work and will make your home smell nice at the same time:

Would you like to receive some beautiful roses? Who wouldn't? Picture those lovely, rich-colored roses in your mind. Bring them to your nose and inhale their sweet scent. Imagine yourself touching the velvety soft petals with your fingertips and gently brushing your cheek against them. Make those roses as real as you possibly can, without actually going out and buying them. Now go about your life, and every so often, when you need a sensual mental break, revisit those roses in your mind.

I guarantee you that those roses will soon appear in your life. Perhaps some client will send them to show appreciation. Maybe you'll be offered a centerpiece from a table arrangement. You'll receive roses as a reminder of an anniversary or an event that you'd completely forgotten about. Or perhaps a friend will have overordered and will give you the extras. Maybe some guy is wooing your best friend with roses, and she doesn't even want to look at them, so she'll give them to you. Or maybe it will be your turn to take home the weekly fresh floral arrangement from your workplace. However they come into your life, I guarantee you that you won't have to wait long. This is an exercise I have the girls in the Millionaire's Club try, and believe it or not, it always works. Just give it a try. What have you got to lose?

The reason it works so well is because you are not in such desperate need of roses. In fact, it's something you would like to have but really don't care that much whether you get them or not. As the Buddhists would say, there is no attachment to the roses, therefore there is no resistance to your receiving them. If, however, it were Valentine's Day and your boyfriend didn't buy you roses, even though all week long you'd been expecting them, it would have been because you blocked them with your resistance.

Divorced? Of Course!

Some of you mistakenly feel that because your marriage(s) ended, you're at a disadvantage. Ladies, nothing could be further from the truth. To be honest, and you know I'm never anything but, divorced girls have a huge advantage. Think about all your invaluable experience! You're not some starry-eyed twenty-something who runs home crying to mommy the first time your husband criticizes you. You know what it takes to make a relationship work, and what will make it crash and burn. You know how to love and how not to love. Men are more likely to look at never-been-married woman over thirty-five and ask, "What's wrong with her?" than they are to say the same thing about a similarly aged woman who is divorced. At least you tried—at least someone picked you. You get big brownie points for this. It sounds harsh to those of us who have never been married, but it's true, and the truth hurts me as much as anyone else, because, as you know, I've never been married. I know what men say about me.

Divorced ladies, for all the trauma and heartbreak you've been through, consider the hard-fought advantages you've won:

1. You're better able to weed out the losers. You've been in the program before, you know all the signs, both good and bad, so you're better able to assess if he'll make a good husband.

2. You can discern his interest level, and your own, much quicker. You don't waste time kidding yourself that this might work if you just give it one more shot. Experience has made you a realist.

3. You're not desperate. You know that, yes, you can recover from a heartbreak, and, no, he's not the last man on earth. You also know that it's better to be alone and happy than in a crappy relationship.

4. Your stock is higher because you've been picked. Men register this in their minds, whether consciously or subconsciously. And if your ex-husband was someone prominent in your community, your stock goes up even higher.

5. You have more realistic expectations. Men love this, because they don't feel the pressure to be perfect. They know that you've seen a man in gross old underwear before and accepted him, warts and all.

These are among the reasons divorced women tend to get married again quicker than a woman of the same age who has never been married. The never-been-married woman deliberates for freaking ever!

However, there is a big difference between the separated woman and the divorced woman. If your divorce is not yet final, chances are you're not quite ready to date yet, because all your issues with your ex have not yet been resolved. You might even still be having ex-sex, so those oxytocin bonds are still binding you to your former husband, and you'll never be able to give it a real shot with anyone new. My advice to the separated woman is to resolve those financial, emotional, and custody issues ASAP so you can move on. You're crazy if you think he'll come back to you once the divorce proceedings have begun. If he initiated the separation, it's likely he was out the door, both emotionally and physically, the second he asked for the split—as a matter of fact, he probably bailed out of the marriage six months prior to that and was just waiting for the right time to tell you. You need to cut your losses and get the hell out of there right away. You might have to give a little in your settlement demands, but that's a good sign that you're over him. Don't waste one more second of your time or your youth on someone who has rejected you. If you've done the rejecting, you're already over him, so why waste any more time? Make the separation period as short as possible, sign the papers, and move on!

Now that you've spent thirty to ninety days in Dating Detox, you'll be cleaner inside than if you'd just gone through a major power colonic, figuratively speaking. You've purged all the bad attitudes, memories, and men from your system, you've found your own happy place, and you're mentally and spiritually ready to move on to the next step. You've made your inner self beautiful; now it's time to do a little (a lot?) of work on your outer self.

STEP TWO

Mirror, Mirror

As you've probably guessed from the title, Step Two involves taking a good long look at yourself, and getting in your ideal dating condition. Now, if you've seen me on *Millionaire Matchmaker*, you know I can be harsh. I tell girls they're too fat or too thin, their hair is too frizzy/curly or the wrong color; I tell them they dress all wrong, or that they act like bitches in heat. Okay, I admit I can be a little rough, but I'm practicing tough love, baby. I'm here to tell you all the things you need to hear, things that even your mother or your sister or your best friend doesn't have the balls to break to you. Let's be real—those women don't have the twenty-plus years of matchmaking experience that I do. They haven't spent half their lives listening to men whine about not being able to find their perfect match. If I had a dollar for every time I heard a man say, "She would be just right if only she would . . ." I'd make Warren Buffett look like a pauper.

So if you feel like you're getting beaten up in this chapter, just know it's for your own good. I'm not making this stuff up—it's based on what thousands of men have told me. You can buck the system and disregard my advice, but don't come crying to me when you don't attract the right guy.

Now, the beauty of Step Two is that it can be going on while you're in Step One and it can continue on into Step Three. This is the time to get your look down, to decide what works best for you and what makes you look and feel like the remarkable diva you are. I promise you that you will feel sexier, skinnier, and superlatively scintillating by the time you're done with this step . . . if you follow my advice.

What's on the Outside DOES Count

Now that you've taken a look at yourself on the inside, it's time to examine the outside: the packaging gives the first impression of all the glory that is you. I hate to say it, but with men, it's all about the packaging—one look is all it takes for them to decide if you're a keeper, or if you should be tossed back. This may sound crude, but they're measuring your "fuckability factor." That's a common term in Hollywood. You've been told this a million times, and it's time you start paying attention to this cold, hard fact. No matter how beautiful you are on the inside, if the outside doesn't reflect it, you're going to spend the rest of your days alone.

As I said, this part of the book will probably be difficult for you, but you're just going to have to suck it up, girlfriend, and take my advice with a grain of salt. It's nothing personal, you understand. I'm just sharing the input men all over the world have shared with me. For some reason, they are comfortable confiding in me. They appreciate my no-nonsense attitude, and they don't sugarcoat anything they say. Believe it or not, they'll tell me things like, "I want her to have boobs just like yours," or, "Yours are too big. I want her to have B's or C's." Think of me as the messenger who spares you the humiliation of having to hear it from the source itself. And, above all, don't shoot the messenger! I'm just passing along the information I gather.

Let's dive right in and discuss your look from head to toe. This is probably what I'm most famous, or infamous, for.

HAIR: If you think you're going to get away with short hair, you're not. Men like long, flowing locks. They just do. The Beckham bob may have been in for twenty seconds, but did you notice Victoria moved on to sporting extensions? I'm a big fan of extensions, as long as they look natural. I often wear them myself. Short, pixie cuts are considered either mannish or over the hill. One prominent celebrity playboy, whose name I can't reveal, told me that when a woman cuts her hair short, it's a sign she's "hit the wall." Her young and sexy days are over. Men appreciate hair they can run their fingers through—and they don't want to get them snagged in scraggly, frizzy, pubic-looking bird's nests. The era of the perm is over, ladies. Wavy hair is fine, but a hair ball is definitely not a man magnet. The money you spend straightening and conditioning your hair might be the best, most profitable investment you'll ever make.

And now a word about color. I outraged a lot of people, and was scourged on internet message boards, for saying on television that "red hair is not the freshest produce on the aisle." Sorry sisters, but it's not. Ninety percent of the men in my club don't pick redheads but go for my assortment of blondes and brunettes. Of course, there *is* that 10 percent who *will* pick a redhead. But many men find red hair startling, and are a little put off to find the carpet matching the bright red drapes. Now, I will say this for you natural redheads—once a man is converted to it, he seldom strays. And there are a number of women who look amazing with red hair: Nicole Kidman, Kate Walsh, Marcia Cross, Debra Messing, and Julianne Moore come to mind—what man wouldn't find those beautiful women attractive? But most of us simply can't pull off red hair in a way that really works for a man.

TEETH: Nothing is more irresistible than a big, white smile. You could be flat as a board, and that smile will draw more attention than all the implants in Beverly Hills. The nice thing about a beautiful white smile is that it's easy to flash and maintain. These days it's also relatively inexpensive to obtain, but put it on credit if you must—this is one area where I say charge it! If your parents didn't invest in orthodontia for you when you were young, run straight to your dentist and see about straightening and whitening your teeth immediately. There are many great options these days, like Lumineers porcelain veneers and Invisalign braces that don't even show, so you no longer need endure ugly railroad tracks. Your smile is your calling card—make sure it's in perfect working order.

LIPS: If your lips are the first thing people notice about your face, they're too big. There's only one Angelina Jolie; stop trying to imitate her, unless you want to end up like Melanie Griffith. If your lips are naturally large, avoid extremely bright or dark lipstick shades. Speaking of lipstick, or lip gloss, don't leave home without it. Always apply it before you set foot outside, even if it's just a quick little swipe. You don't have to do the entire lip lining procedure, but a little color and shine make you look young and fresh and approachable. Also, try a good lip plumper—it's an inexpensive tool that will work every time and not inflate your lips to duck bill proportions. Why not put your best lip forward?

MAKEUP: Less is more. I know, women on TV and in the movies appear to pile it on, but that's only necessary for the cameras and harsh lighting. I admit to being guilty as charged. But in everyday life, I'm a bronzer and lip gloss girl, period. The only people who successfully smear on layers of makeup are drag queens. Most straight men prefer their mates to have a low-maintenance look anyway. You might spend an hour achieving it, but your man loves you to appear as natural as possible. And whatever you do, don't cake on the foundation. A little lipstick or gloss, blush, eyeliner, and mascara can easily do the trick. If you're uncertain about how to apply makeup, set up an appointment with a makeup artist at a salon, or go to an upscale cosmetics line representative in a mall or a department store—you don't even have to buy anything. One of my favorite places to spend time is Sephora, because they carry so many different lines of makeup that you're sure to find your perfect match, and they give samples! Be extremely careful about whom you pick to do your makeup, however. Avoid the women who look like clowns, or the gay men wearing makeup. Never let a gay man tell you how to be a better woman—he'll never understand exactly what it's like to be an attractive female looking for a hetero-sexual male.

SKIN CARE: The real secret to great-looking makeup is great-looking skin. I'd suggest seeing your dermatologist to find a regimen that works for you. As far as procedures go, I like microdermabrasions, oxygen facials, Vi Peel, and Aluma skin treatments. I don't like to waste money, so I check out all the latest fads extensively before I indulge. I've been using La Prairie skin care products for twenty years, and I always break out when I try the hot, new fad, so I figure if it ain't broke, don't fix it. I mean, do I look like a forty-seven-year-old woman? I think not.

I've never used Botox, but I'm considering it. I'm cer-tainly not against it, although I'd advise you to run away from any kind of an injection party. Think about it: There is usually alcohol at those events, and do you really want to be making decisions about your face when you're tipsy? Are you going to give credence to the opinions of your drunken friends? What about the person who's doing the injecting? Has he/she been drinking? People end up looking like Category Five hurricanes after those things, and they're horrified when they wake up the next morning. You should do all your skin care consulting in the light of day, in the privacy of an office, alone with a doctor and/or nurse who will be focused on you, not on socializing. If the doctor suggests a number of procedures above and beyond what you came in for, be wary. Take your time. Look at before and after pictures. Check your doctor's credentials and get references. Keep in mind that just as the cheapest might not be the best, the most expensive might not be either.

And while we're on the subject of skin, don't forget to pay attention to your neck and hands. They show age and abuse quicker than anything. Use plenty of lotion, both day and night, and don't forget the sunscreen. Manicures and good nail care are essential. Professional nail care is so inexpensive these days, and men think beautifully manicured hands are very sexy.

Also, remember to take your makeup off, cleanse your skin, and use night cream every night, no exceptions. I don't care if you're tired—do you want a husband or not?

BODY: Here it comes! Stop holding your breath and exhale. The good news is that there's not one certain body type that all men adore. There are breast men, leg men, ass men—even foot men, although they tend to be a little kinky.

The perfect body is all about attitude, really. If you love your body, you're probably in the best shape you could possibly be. Most women, myself included, have big, debilitating issues about body image. I know very few women who can honestly say, "I feel fabulous, and I love my body." As a matter of fact, I don't know any woman who can say that with a straight face. We all want to lose those extra ten pounds. We all want to get rid of those perceived pouches and love handles, even if no one else can see them. We all perk up when we hear of a new diet or health food that promises to melt away the pounds. And we've all stayed home some night because we felt like we looked like gross pigs. It's hard being a female in today's airbrushed, supermodel society. But the good news is that there's hope. We can change things.

I hate to sound cliché, but exercise and nutrition are the best ways to change the way you look and feel. How much better do you feel after taking a hike and eating a crunchy salad than after watching two hours of TV and helping yourself to a steaming pile of chili cheese fries? You want to feel sleek and sexy, not bloated and lethargic. The lighter you feel and weigh, the sexier you feel. And it takes a different regime for each of us to achieve that. It works for me to follow one simple rule: If I eat, I've gotta walk. If I want to indulge in my favorite food, I need to walk it off. No ifs, ands, or big butts.

I'm also a big fan of colonics and cleanses (don't call them enemas), although they can get addictive and overdone. These days it's not uncommon for a group of women to treat themselves to a good colonic, the way they used to socialize over facials, manies, and pedies. It's super for detoxifying your body after an overindulgent vacation, at the beginning of a new diet, after a bad breakup, or before a big event. It really makes you feel fresh and new to shed all those nasty toxins that are clawing around inside you. Make sure you go to a clean, reputable place that has the latest equipment, and get references. A good colonist will make sure that you are relaxed, feeling safe, and will adjust the pressure of the machine to accommodate you.

Crash diets can be helpful to kick-start a weight-loss program, but the quick five pounds you lose for that class reunion or wedding will come right back unless you actually change your eating habits. I've tried every diet out there, and they've helped me to lose a lot of weight in record time, but the weight always comes back unless I make a long-term commitment to stick to food that's fresh, healthy, fibrous, low carb, high protein, and unprocessed. I can't recommend one diet or way of eating for everyone, because no two metabolisms are alike.

But the best nutritionist in the world will go to waste if you don't couple your fitness efforts with a good exercise program. Exercise not only makes you look better, but also feel better, as we discussed in Step One. Find something that works for you, that you actually enjoy. Maybe try swimming, spinning, dancing, boxing, or walking your dog. A lot of women are having fun and meeting men in mixed martial arts classes, which are also great for developing self-discipline. Make sure you stick with it, however, until you experience that intoxicating endorphin rush that accompanies a hard workout. I swear, exercise can be better than sex . . . okay, at least better than sex with a guy who doesn't love you. And exercise is far cleaner and less complicated.

If you feel you've tried everything you've ever read or researched on the internet, and you still haven't slimmed down, it might be time to consult the professionals. Make an appointment with a highly recommended personal trainer, a nutritionist, or, ideally, find someone who qualifies as both, so that you can coordinate your exercise and eating habits. There are plenty of inexpensive internet sites that you can join and consult with daily, but it might be worth your while to make a substantial monetary investment in this so that you'll be more inclined to stick with it.

What a Waist!

Here's a little added incentive to get your butt up on the treadmill. Did you know that if you only lose an inch or two off your waist and hips, you could easily find yourself sporting what has classically been considered the perfect figure? Many studies have been done on this. It doesn't matter how big or how slender you are, if your waist measurement is 70 percent of your hip measurement, men will think you're hotter. Women with body types as diverse as Marilyn Monroe and Gong Li are reported to have the 0.7 waist-hip ratio. Even the Venus de Milo, for centuries considered the epitome of beauty, has it. Go figure—literally.

You can figure out your own waist to hip ratio by taking a tape measure and measuring around the smallest part of your waist. Write that number down. Now measure around the largest part of your hips (go around your butt, not your thighs). Divide your waist measurement by your hip measurement. So if your waist measurement is 27, and you divide that by your 41-inch hip measurement, rounded off you've got the perfect 0.7 waist-to-hip ratio! And get this, ladies—those measurements are not just for those who are a size 2—they also apply to a healthy size 8. It's all about proportion.

There are many ways to adjust your figure to that perfect ratio even if you're simply not curvaceous. If you're willing to buy yourself a padded push-up bra, why not buy padded push-up jeans or shapers that you can wear under your clothes? They even make bathing suits with butt padding. At the very least, you can wear clothes that emphasize and enhance your curves, like a simple black belt around your waist.

Your New Best Friends

Now, even if you're eating like The Biggest Loser and working out as if Jillian Michaels were cracking a whip over your head, you can always use a little extra help. I'm going to fill you in on a little secret that will slim you down two sizes in five minutes—I'm not kidding. I promise you, if you don't get one other thing out of this book, this and this alone will make you feel like you got your money's worth. Get ready to meet your new best friend: shapewear.

We're not talking about your grandmother's girdle; shapewear has come a long way over the past couple of years. It doesn't matter if you're Kate Moss or Queen Latifah, we all have our wobbly bits, as Bridget Jones likes to call them. Even the best-bodied stars, like Jessica Alba, Beyoncé, Salma Hayek, and Nicole Kidman admit to using a little extra help when walking the red carpet. I accidentally stumbled across their secret recently when I was shopping for clothes for my television appearances.

If you saw the first season of *Millionaire Matchmaker*, you might recall those horribly unflattering baby doll dresses wardrobe made me wear. Since they don't show you daily film clips when you're doing a reality show, I had no idea those dresses and tops made me look so much larger than life until the actual show aired, and I was horrified. There was no way I was going to wear those things when I made appearances to promote the show, several months later. I mean, who wants to appear on *Ellen* and *Tyra* and *Today* looking like a forty-seven-year-old pregnant woman? So I raced to Nordstrom and told them I needed form-fitting dresses, tops, and skirts that would show off my assets and minimize my flaws. "No problem," said the savvy salesclerk. Before she stocked me up on beautiful wrap dresses and pencil skirts, she whisked me by the lingerie department, where she introduced me to the wonderful world of shapewear. The items she had me try on not only whittled away two sizes as soon as I wriggled into them but they were actually comfortable and made me feel sleeker and sexier.

There is shapewear to hide every flaw. There are slips to smooth the bulges on your butt, thighs, and tummy. There are form-fitting tights and shorts of every length to make you look your best in pants. There is even long-sleeve shapewear to keep you warm and to control the chicken-wing look. My favorite is a full-length shaper that has lace at the décolletage. It lifts my butt, flattens my tummy, gives me support, minimizes my bust, and looks sexy when the lace peaks out of a low-cut neckline. It also has a hole at the crotch so that I don't have to get undressed when I pee. I even bought one for my mother, who's in her seventies. Since she comes from the age of the girdle, she especially loves it. Both Oprah and Tyra admit to being shapewear fans.

If you're worried about what your man will think when you're alone together and the moment of truth arrives and it's time to shed your shaper, I say, fear not! Once it's dark and he's smelling you, touching you, feeling you, he'll never notice the difference.

Seriously, my friends, if you don't have any shapewear yet, I'd say run, don't walk, down to the nearest department store and try some on for size. You can thank me later.

And if this makes you work up a sweat, here's a new secret weapon I received from my stylists, Joanne and Marni. It's called Certain Dri. It's a deodorant you put on before you go to bed at night, and you'll never sweat again. I used to not be able to wear silk to any event because I risked ugly sweat stains. I even considered getting Botox in my armpits, but I hate needles, so I was ecstatic to find this deodorant. And get this, ladies—you don't even have to use it every night. It lasts for seventy-two hours. Believe me, I've been shooting in the heat of an LA summer, and you'll never see me sweat on camera.

Shop 'til You Pop

Speaking of shopping, during Step Two you get to go on a little shopping spree. During Dating Detox you cleaned out your closet so you have room for more clothes, and since you're not wasting money on junk food any more, you'll find you have a few extra dollars in your purse. Even if the budget is tight, it's important that you find some way to cover a new dating wardrobe. The clothes you own now are obviously not working, or you wouldn't be reading this book. Think of it as an investment in your future.

What types of clothes should you buy? Look for clothes that make you feel like the sexy diva you are. Men are drawn to women who are comfortable in their own femininity and know how to show it. I'm not talking about pastel-colored ruffles and lace—that's far too fussy and old-fashioned. No, I'm talking about showing off your assets. Buy skirts that show off your gorgeous legs if you have them, or seductively cut tops that enhance your cleavage. Solid, bright colors are guaranteed Guy Catchers, but not big prints that will distract him. Also, stay away from black, unless you want to fade into the woodwork.

Everyone wears black these days—sure, it's chic and hides all sorts of flaws, but it's also boring and unoriginal. Colors like red and blue will draw him in. Fitted clothes will keep him there. You don't want to wear clothes that are so tight you bulge out of them, but you do want to show off your figure, so steer clear of anything baggy or blousy (and don't forget about the shapewear). Look through some fashion magazines or catalogs to find styles and colors you think might look good on you.

Now it's time to make a date to go shopping, and you must go with one person in particular. Not your mother or your sister or your best friend—they might not be honest with you. Not your favorite gay guy, no matter how much style and how many opinions he seems to have. Again, gay men don't know how to attract straight men. Since you're after the single straight man, you guessed it—go shopping with a single, straight man.

It could be your brother, your cousin, a colleague from the office, your best friend from school, the concierge in your building, for that matter—even your ex-boyfriend, but only if you're not still attracted to him. He just better be straight and actively dating. Stay away from the nerd who never goes out—he'll advise you to dress like a tramp.

When you're walking the racks with your new shopping partner, ask him, "How would you like me to dress if I were your girlfriend? What would turn you on?" So that you don't impose or overwhelm him, limit your shopping trip to two hours, and make sure you treat him to something he likes afterward, like a beer and a burger at a sports bar. It's best to pick a mall or a densely populated shopping area so you don't have to waste valuable time driving between stores. Have him help you select three or four outfits, including some killer classic jeans, a great dress, a couple of cute tops, and a flattering skirt.

If there's time, let him help you select some shoes, and don't be surprised or complain when he picks out stilettos. Men LOVE a woman in heels. Four-inch heels are the new standard. It's worth the investment to buy a pair that are comfortable, yet sexy. The whole point is to get attention.

These new clothes will be invaluable. You'll wear the clothes he helps you select not only on dates, but when you're out and about on the town attracting men into your circle. You'll seldom feel more luscious than when you're wearing the clothes your best straight male friend helped you select.

Sexy Is as Sexy Does

No doubt about it, if you *feel* sexy, you're more inclined to *look* sexy. Sexy is a confident, fun loving, happy, sensuous, approachable state of mind that no man can resist. Even gay and married men are attracted to a sexy, savvy, sensual woman, so you'll have to exercise discretion when you let your inner sexy out—you may be so overwhelmed with male attention that Mr. Right won't be able to make his way through the crowd.

Now, if all this talk of sexiness makes you uncomfortable because you've never really explored your sensual side, or you never really thought of yourself as "that kind of girl," I'm going to give you the keys to finding your own inner sexy. If you're a female with her sex organs intact, there's gotta be some sexy down in there somewhere, and I'm going to help you bring it to the surface. You don't have to be the classic brazen bombshell for men to be attracted to you in "that way." You could be any of the following types:

CUTE AND PERKY: This is the cheerleader in high school who all the boys adored. Think of Kelly Ripa, Reese Witherspoon, Kristen Bell, Jessica Simpson, Elisabeth Hasselbeck, Drew Barrymore, and Kristin Chenoweth. She's often blonde but could be brunette as well. Her perkiness sometimes annoys other women, but men love her upbeat, lively attitude.

PATTI STANGER

Men who are most attracted to this type are the former jocks in high school who remain physically active after graduation. They have to have a lot of energy to keep up with this one! Men who gravitate toward perky women are generally adventurers and explorers, and they're highly sociable. They have a lot of friends and maybe a dog as well. They love to entertain with a perky hostess at their side, and they're extremely well liked wherever they go. They will forgive a perky woman if she's not a perfect 10, because they worship her optimism and enthusiasm. They know and value the fact that the perky woman smiles in times of crisis, and stands by her man no matter what.

THE GIRL NEXT DOOR: She grew up under everyone's radar, was possibly a tomboy in high school, but one day emerged as a classic beauty with a radiant smile. Jennifer Garner, Jennifer Aniston, Cameron Diaz, Cindy Crawford, Kristin Davis, Téa Leoni, Scarlett Johansson, Christie Brinkley, Katherine Heigl, and Hilary Swank are all girls next door. She probably got good grades and was athletic, played volleyball, tennis, water polo, volleyball, or field hockey, and continues to be athletic well into her adult years. Athletic men who use sports to climb the corporate ladder are attracted to her. They love her natural beauty and will not encourage her to get plastic surgery. Men who marry the Girl Next Door usually have good jobs and high standing in the community. Theirs will be a good, healthy, more traditional relationship, because they share the same values. They could share and be active in a religion. Men who are attracted to the Girl Next

Door are looking for someone they can hang out with rather than the perfect 10. These are not the girls they have affairs with, but the girls they end up marrying, although they may take their time in proposing.

SEXPOT: She exudes sensuality at the exclusion of everything else—it's the first thing you think of when you see her. Marilyn Monroe epitomized this, and today we have Pamela Anderson, Carmen Electra, Britney Spears, Milla Jovovich, Madonna, Christina Aguilera, Mariah Carey, and Kim Cattrall, to name a few. Her business and career are often based on something having to do with sex. They've got "it," and they're not afraid to flaunt it, much to almost every man's delight. Sexpots attract all types of men, and nerdish types are absolutely fanatical about them, although they seldom end up with them. Sexpots need to be careful, because it's often the flashy players who come after them full force and snare them, but they'll have tumultuous, short-lived relationships together. New money and big spenders who quickly squander everything want the Sexpot on their arm, to prove what their money can do, and Sexpots get proposals quicker than any other type. If Sexpots don't use their heads, they can easily end up as trophy wives. Since Sexpots are the object of every man's fantasy, they're constantly under pressure to sleep with a man too soon, and they often feel used because men want to be inside their bodies, but don't really care what's inside their hearts or heads. Think of the poor, sad choices in men made by both Marilyn Monroe and Britney Spears. Sexpots are always complaining about not being taken seriously. It's a good idea for a Sexpot to establish herself and excel in some other area—career, charity work, motherhood, research, etc., so that she won't be thought of exclusively as a sex object, and so that, when gravity and age take hold, she's not left with nothing but sagging boobs and butt. Not everyone can be a Sophia Lauren, who will be a classy Sexpot until the day she dies.

EXOTIC: These women are arresting because there is something unusual and intriguing about them—they may not be considered classically beautiful, but their features are presented in a unique way. They define their own class of beauty. Penélope Cruz, Shakira, Uma Thurman, Eva Longoria, Halle Berry, Angelina Jolie, Gong Li, Salma Hayek, Iman, Lucy Liu, and Tyra Banks are perfect examples of this type of sexy. As you can see, they can be any ethnicity, except for your standard all-American. Men who are their polar opposites are often attracted to Exotics. It's up to the Exotic woman to decide if she wants a mate who has a common culture, or just the opposite. She can make it work with either one, if she can just get past the mother-in-law. She must also be strong enough to capitalize on the best of both cultures to help her children with the challenges they may face. If she can find the perfect balance, she can have the perfect relationship. Her husband tends to be very loyal.

INTELLECTUAL: In the Millionaire's Club this is the type of woman most requested but hardest to find. One of my clients put it this way: "Any idiot can be sexy, but a really whip-smart woman, especially someone who has achieved success based on her brain power, now that's REALLY sexy." Think of Gwyneth Paltrow, Natalie Portman, Brooke Shields, Anne Curry, Meredith Vieira, Bianna Golodryga, Maureen Dowd, Arianna Huffington, Tina Fey, Maria Bartiromo, Katharine Hepburn, Lauren Bacall, Carly Fiorina, Sherry Lansing, Kathy Freston, Maria Shriver, and Marianne Williamson. Yes, they're all beautiful, but they lead with their intellectual foot. They use their brains to enhance their beauty, and often radiate class and elegance. To the intelligent, cultured male, brains are sexy. The Intellectual's beauty is not forced, neither are her brains. They are smart enough to be confident and composed. They're comfortable in their femininity and understand that a skirt and heels can be the ultimate power suit. It takes an intelligent, successful, confident man to please an Intellectual woman, but unfortunately, these types of men are somewhat hard to come by. The Intellectual woman should look for an older man, because it takes men longer to develop the level of success and confidence she'll find compatible. Theirs will be a slow-burning relationship—interest will rise with witty verbal ping-pong and intellectual sparring. A man will take his time in proposing to an Intellectual woman, because he wants everything to be perfect with her, and he fears her disapproval. Her greatest challenge in a relationship is giving her partner sufficient attention and respect. No man (or woman) enjoys coming in second to a career, and it's very hard to switch gears suddenly. Intellectual women can also be cynical, overanalytical, and judgmental if they're not careful—they're accustomed to trusting their heads, not their hearts.

Ask yourself which category you fall in. Once you decide, work it, baby! Google the women I've mentioned in your category, and see how they dress, act, and manage their lives. Pay attention to the mistakes they've made as well as their successes. Decide what they're doing that you're not that might be keeping you from maximizing your sexiness.

And while we're on the subject of maximizing your sexiness, know that there will be times when you just can't get it up, so to speak. No one feels scrumptious and scintillating 24–7. For this reason, I've provided you with the following list of quick, sexy fixes. Try any of them right before you go out, and you'll be thrilled with the difference they can make:

- Go to a salon and have your hair washed and styled or blown out.
- Get a bikini wax.
- Have a long, relaxing massage.
- Have your makeup done in a department store.
- Bathe with your favorite scented bath gel, then use the lotion in a matching scent.
- Dance around the house naked, listening to your favorite music.
- Wear a lacy matching bra and panties.
- Wear a dress or skirt with no panties at all.
- Have a glass of champagne as you're getting ready.
- Put a removable tattoo on your inner thigh.
- Wear a long strand of pearls. Put them on first, and

look at yourself in the mirror wearing nothing but the pearls.

- Buy a pair of spiky stilettos and practice strutting in them.
- Wear sheer, black thigh-high stockings under your skirt.
- Apply false eyelashes.
- Listen to sensual music as you prepare to go out. My favorites include Gato Barbieri's "Europa" and Joe Cocker's "You Can Leave Your Hat On."
- Pleasure yourself right before you leave (this gives you a scintillating glow and keeps you from feeling desperate for sex).

If you're not confident with your inner sexy yet, take it out for a test drive. Give a seductive smile to the parking attendant. Walk into your favorite coffee shop in your stilettos. Go to work one day in a flowing skirt with no panties. Take baby steps. No one blossoms into the ultimate seductress overnight. Little by little, you will notice men looking at you longer than they did before. When you walk into a room and you sense masculine eyes focusing in your direction, you'll turn around to see who they're looking at and be surprised to find no one there—they're staring at you! You'll start getting better service in stores and restaurants from men, and you'll note that guys are offering to do extra favors for you when they have nothing more to gain than your approving smile.

There is nothing cheap, brazen, or kinky about reveling in

your sexiness. It is an inherent part of your nature, and to live a full life, you need to become comfortable with it. Even my mother enjoys feeling sexy and attractive. Her vibe has changed a bit since she was in her prime, of course, but as I mentioned, men are still approaching her constantly. And rather than resenting it, my dad gets a kick out of it. All men like to feel that their woman is desired by others.

Now that you've made the most of what you've got and raised your desirability factor to the highest degree, it's time to zero in on your target. The man of your dreams is out there, waiting to be overwhelmed by your feminine charms, and I'm going to show you where to find him.

Make Your Own Matchmaking Map

The three most important factors in finding your perfect match are a lot like the three most important factors in finding your perfect house: location, location, location! To make the best use of your time and effort, it's helpful to know where the single men congregate, both nationally and locally. There might be a hidden bunker brimming with them right in your own backyard. You just have to know where to look. You'll also need to know where your competition is the hottest so you can avoid those places. Who wants to compete against nubile, twenty-four-year-old hotties, unless, of course, you're a nubile, twenty-two-year-old hottie? Since the Millionaire's Club is international, I've been able to make fascinating and often surprising observations about where the men are the most marriage minded, and where they wouldn't commit to you even if you were a sweet, young, natural 34-D heiress with a PhD.

First, let's talk geography. You've heard horror stories about the ratio of single women to single men in the US, but actually the numbers are not so bad. There are only about 6 percent more single women than single men. There are approximately 25.4 million single guys in the US that are between the ages of twenty-five and fifty-four, which is quite a few to choose from, but it's the concentration of singles in any given area that is more important to consider. Are you living in an area that is geographically desirable for the marriage minded? A US Singles Map was published in the *Boston Globe* that confirmed the stats that I've always believed to be true.

Cities where single men outnumber women by at least 40,000: Los Angeles/Orange County, San Francisco, Seattle, Las Vegas, Phoenix, Dallas-Fort Worth, Austin, and Houston.

However, a note of caution: These numbers are misleading when it comes to the Los Angeles/Orange County area, where there are approximately 89,459 more single men than single women. Those may sound like good numbers, but don't load up the truck and move to Beverly just yet. The sad truth about Southern California is that the most beautiful women in the world gravitate toward LA on a daily basis. You see gorgeous women—what I call tits on a stick—they're even parking your damn car. You really can't blame a guy for noticing all this eye candy, but the problem is, LA is the land where the zero male can get a 10 female and still think he can do better. So California men use the rest of us mere mortal women, who aren't the sought-after supermodels, for sex while they wait for Paris Hilton to fall into their laps.

If you've been fishing in the Southern California pond for some time and haven't found a keeper yet, I'd suggest moving to another city where the numbers are still in your favor, and where they're more forgiving of physical imperfection. A woman who is fifteen pounds overweight can throw on the sweats, put on some blush, and she'll be considered ravishing in Chicago. She'll have a date every night in Minneapolis or Seattle, but she'll sit home alone for months in LA

There are other places to avoid as well, statistically speaking. The cities with at least 40,000 more single women than single men are: New York/northern New Jersey, Memphis, Atlanta, Philadelphia, and Washington DC.

The New York/northern New Jersey area has approximately 185,000 more single women than single men. That boils down to about 81 single men for every 100 single women in New York City. I don't like those odds. Not at all. If it's possible for you to do the job you love in some other city, I'd suggest moving there. If this appears desperate to you, look at it this way: You wouldn't bat an eyelash about relocating to a different city for professional reasons—if you got a transfer, or if the job market were better for your particular career, in, say, Dallas, you'd feel fine about moving there, right? So what's the problem with moving somewhere to find true love? It lasts a lot longer and is infinitely more satisfying than any job you'll ever have.

Now, the above information is based on the singles population only. Different publications are always doing studies on the best US cities for singles. I particularly like the research *Forbes* has done, because they base their studies not only on the percentage of the population that's single in each city, but they also take into consideration factors such as activities conducive to dating, divorce rates, fitness levels, and education levels. So I'd suggest checking out their survey and other recent ones.

Mapping Out Your Time and Efforts

It's important to work smart during your search. As with your investment portfolio—what do you mean you don't have one? Get one. NOW. Forego new shoes, jeans, and cigarettes for the next three months and you'll have a decent nest egg to invest. As I was saying, as with a good investment portfolio, you don't want to put all your eggs in one basket. You want to spread your efforts around, so if one road dead-ends, you'll have plenty of other avenues to cruise. I'd suggest dividing your time equally between the following three endeavors:

1. **Online:** There's no shame anymore in meeting people on internet dating sites. It expands your options worldwide and allows you to meet people you'd never come in contact with otherwise.
2. **Personal Contacts:** A great way to meet eligible singles is through friends, family, or professional matchmakers. Not only do these guys come pretested and vetted, but you'll know how to track them down and punish them if they do you wrong.
3. **Out and About:** It's important to do some of the heavy lifting yourself, by going to strategic locations to rub

shoulders with the kind of single man you love most. Don't get apprehensive—I'll give you plenty of suggestions for locations and how to work them.

Doing Fine Online

Conduct your online search for a match just like you'd conduct an online job search. Post an honest, flawless profile highlighting your assets, and don't take it personally if a particularly interesting prospect fails to contact you. He might have recently gotten involved with someone else and not removed his profile yet, he might be flooded with other options, or maybe he identified something in your profile that he feels is a deal breaker. That's okay—if that's the case, you don't want to waste time with him anyway.

Internet dating should be fun. If it becomes a burdensome, boring, or bitter experience, simply ditch it. Remember, you're supposed to enjoy the whole dating process. You don't want to be so burned out, stressed, and jumpy over the process that you snap, "What the hell do YOU want?" when Mr. Right taps you on the shoulder. We've all been in that space.

One of the most important things for a woman to remember about internet dating is that under no circumstances should you contact a man first. You must ALWAYS wait for him to contact you. Now, don't go all postal on me for saying this. There are exceptions to every rule, of course, and you might have even experienced one. It's just that online, as in the real world, men like to be the hunters, the aggressors—

they like to make the first move. If you make the first move, you take all the joy out of the hunt for him. Either that, or you establish yourself as the aggressor, and he'll let you take on that role throughout the relationship. What woman wants to take the initiative all the time? That's no fun!

I found this out the hard way. When I was new to online dating, I came across the profile of a hot, handsome, older television producer who had rippling muscles, and I've always had a weakness for that. He was also a homeowner, which is always a plus with me. I naïvely sent him a note inviting him to check out my profile. He did, liked what he saw, we exchanged a few emails, and decided to meet for drinks. The date went phenomenally well. Drinks progressed to dinner, and we ended up closing the restaurant down. I thought he was the one. He paid the valet, and then, as he was driving away, he rolled down his window and said, "Call me."

That certainly let the air out of my love balloon. I don't initiate calls to men. Ever. I was well trained at the Rhoda Goldstein School of Dating. Mom told me to let them call me, and I stick to that. So days went by and he didn't call. I was extremely disappointed, because we really seemed to have something going. Much to my surprise, several weeks later I ran into him at a party, and seething with curiosity I went against my own intuition and asked him, "What happened?"

"*You* picked *me* on the internet, *you* should chase *me*," he said.

At that point I almost started to vomit. That was the end of that. I don't chase men, under any circumstances. Even though he was a lazy California guy, I learned once again that a woman has to let the man be the aggressor—even online.

Picture Perfect

To get a better man, you need a better photo. So how do you lure men to your profile and get them to make the first move? First of all, you need to have a fabulous, *professional* photo taken. I insist on professional photographs for the girls in my club because pros have plenty of experience with making people look their best on camera. No amateur can rival a professional's skill with lighting and angles. You'll be amazed at how beautiful you can look through the lens of a professional. Plus, having pictures taken and getting you hair and makeup done for the shoot makes you feel wonderful—it's a tremendous ego boost.

Now, specifically, you need to post at least one three-quarter length shot, from the top of your head to below your thighs. Headshots are fine when presented with a mix of photos, but if you only show your face, many guys assume you're hiding an unattractive body. A man wants to see the whole package—don't you? Don't wear something trendy—you'll want to be able to use these photos for up to five years if you don't change your weight or hair. Simple, form-fitting dresses work well—no blousy, trapeze, or baby doll dresses allowed. If you have bad arms, wear long sleeves, but if you have hot yoga arms, break out the tank. A push-up bra is essential. Also, have the photographer shoot several photos of you in a classy, solid-color, form-fitting top, like a T-shirt, and solid dark jeans (they make you look thinner than light jeans).

The most important thing of all to wear in your pictures is a smile; it's what will win his heart instantly. Don't try to look sultry, contemplative, far away, or thoughtful. Don't play the vixen, looking like you're about to bite off his penis. Your calling card is your smile, so make sure you use whitening strips before your shoot. You need to appear engaging, inviting, warm, and happy. Men find this most attractive of all.

Have your hair and makeup done professionally—not by your best friend. If you think you can do it yourself, trust me, you will not show up well on camera, especially a digital camera, which is what almost all photographers use these days. And one more thing: I know I sound like a broken record, but if you have curly or wavy hair, get it blown out straight and silky for your photo shoot. It's worth paying the money once a year to get it thermal reconditioned, also known as Japanese straightening.

Professional photos, hair and makeup shouldn't cost more than $350–$500, depending upon your city. It's usually more expensive in big cities. The photographer's price should include one or two photos with free touch-ups, and will probably be more if you want additional photos retouched. Just as Botox is essential for wrinkles when you're past thirty-five, retouching is essential for photos. That may sound like a lot of money, but it's one of the best investments in your future that you'll ever make. Besides, you'll get a lot of mileage out of those photos. You can put them on your résumé, your MySpace or Facebook page, you can give them to family members for Christmas and birthdays, and you can use them for another great purpose I'll tell you about later in this chapter.

Photo PS: Never post a photo of yourself with a drink in your hand—it will attract alcoholics. And never post a photo of yourself with another man, thinking they'll be impressed by how attractive you are. Hunter males are turned off by you waving the competition in their faces. They don't have time for games.

Provocative Profile

Now it's time to write a happy, flirty, fun profile. It helps to pick out a provocative, flattering screen name. I used to get a lot of mileage out of Sultry Brunette, Bi-coastal Beauty, and Sugar and Spice. Lisa went on JDate (the international website for Jewish singles) as Low Maintenance, and was deluged with attention, for reasons that if you don't understand, I'm not going to explain. Why not try putting a "'licious" at the end of your name, such as Lindalicious, or describe your best feature, such as Velvet Voiced Vixen or Blue-eyed Bella? After your photo, your screen name will be the second thing he'll notice about you, and it will either attract or repel him. Whatever you do, don't give yourself a cutesy screen name that focuses on something else, such as Kitty Lover or Brandon's Mommy. This profile is all about you—don't divert his attention.

When writing about yourself in the meat of the profile, don't state your intentions or desires first. Catch his attention with what you have to offer. Lead with your strengths, and don't worry about being humble. This is your time to shine! Use exciting words, such as playful, energetic, fun, upbeat, positive, fit, creative, attractive, and sharp. Stay away from words that are too sexual, like sexy, steamy, and sensuous. Those are code words for "I'm looking for a quickie." Use adjectives that describe your character and your physical appearance. Then move on to describing your profession, and transition into writing about what you're looking for. There are subtle ways to say, "I want to find a husband as soon as possible," without appearing desperate. Try, "Let's grow old together." Or "I would like to share my wonderful life with one special guy."

Now let's be brutally honest here: we'd almost all like to find a wealthy husband—who doesn't want to be financially secure, enjoy the better things in life, and not have to constantly struggle and fight about money? But you don't want to come across as a gold digger in your profile, and that's hard to avoid. There's one word that scares the hell out of men, no matter what their financial status. That word is "generous." Never say, "I'm looking for a generous man who will . . ." or any variation on that theme. Men will get the message that you're seeking an upscale type if you say something like, "Looking for a guy at the top of his game," "Hoping to find someone who loves his work and is successful." Or, "I'm doing great in my career, and I hope you are too." You can also list upscale interests you enjoy, such as fine wine and gourmet dining, golf, tennis, or boating. Above all, never write that you're interested in "shopping." Most straight, marriage-minded men do not enjoy shopping with you. You might think this is a no-brainer, but you would be surprised how many times it comes up when I interview women for the Millionaire's Club.

It's also a good idea to open yourself up to a bigger playing field in your profile. Think about your boundaries for what is geographically desirable, and try expanding them by at least one hundred miles. I know, it can be really difficult to date someone eighty miles away if you live in a major metropolitan area where there's extreme traffic, like Los Angeles or Atlanta, but if you're really looking for The One, **love knows no distance**. If business takes you to another city fairly often, consider dating people there. My friend Carol, for example, lives in Manhattan where there are plenty of prospects for her, but she opened herself up to dates with men in New Jersey, Philly, Connecticut, and Florida. She's had two great, long-term relationships with men in the Philadelphia area, and she finds this ideal because she usually works about sixty-five hours per week and loves to go out of town on the weekends for recreation.

Also, don't write off the men you meet on vacation, even if they live far away (which they probably will). Long-distance relationships tend to go faster because of the "I miss you" factor. Plus, if he's from a cold state, it's especially beneficial to find him on a sunny, beach vacation. He's out of his cold-weather, buttoned-down clothes, he's happy and carefree and open to romance. There's a good reason everyone flocks down to Florida for spring break.

Honesty Is the Best Policy

The most important thing to remember about presenting yourself online is to be absolutely, 100 percent honest. Both males and females agree that the number one problem with finding a date on the internet is the lack of honesty. People post photos taken fifteen years ago when they were twenty-five pounds lighter and had a full head of hair. People can lie about their ages, their professions, even their marital status. You'll find a lot of men who write that they're divorced when they're still living with their wives and just toying with the idea of separating—unbeknownst to their spouses. I'll never forget the time an attorney came to pick me up for the fourth date in a minivan full of kids' paraphernalia and fast-food wrappers. I missed his Porsche, and asked him what had happened to it.

"It's in the shop," he told me. "This is my second car."

I ask you: what kind of guy drives a minivan as a second car? It was obviously a mommy 'mobile, and I've never known an ex-wife who would loan her husband her car for a date. "You're still living at home, and this is your wife's car, isn't it?" I accused.

"Well . . ." he said sheepishly. "You got me. I *am* still living at home, but my wife and I haven't slept together in months."

Right. Why do men always expect you to believe that line, "We haven't slept together in months," as if that's going to make everything all right? My answer? "See ya!"

If the object of internet dating is to meet and begin a relationship, realize that you'll have to come face-to-face with this person sooner or later, so you might as well 'fess up in the beginning. If you're fifteen pounds overweight, you can say you're "zaftig," "Rubenesque" or "curvaceous." A man who is into the anorexic waif types is not going to be attracted to you anyway, so why even bother meeting? Why lie about your age when your childbearing years might be a huge issue? You're not only wasting time and effort, but you're compromising your integrity. You're lying, cheating, and deceiving. I don't really think you're that type of person, are you? Many women cling desperately to the belief that "If he could just spend some time with me face-to-face, my charming personality will convince him to overlook all those extra pounds." It's a nice thought, but it ain't gonna happen, sister. Remember, the penis does the picking. If a man wants a skinnier woman, a younger woman, a taller woman, whatever, nothing you can do or say is going to make him change his mind. Stop kidding yourself. Get in the best shape you possibly can, own up to your beautiful age, and be honest about it! There ARE men out there who don't care so much about your age or weight. (They just don't live in Los Angeles.)

Relationship in Bloom

So you post this scintillating profile and fabulous photos, and within twenty-four hours you are deluged with messages from potential dates. Don't be surprised by this. Most online dating services alert people within twenty-four hours when someone new who meets their criteria joins. You want to make the most of your first week and month, because you're considered fresh meat, and that's when you'll get the most attention. You'll also be first on their photo rotation of new, attractive women. They always need the pretty ones to highlight. You'll probably have so many contacts you won't know where to start. It's important to delete the undesirables quickly, because they can actually fill up your mailbox and crash it so that it doesn't allow any more real contenders to contact you. How do you weed them out? Here's a list of men worthy of the delete key:

1. Men who give you their phone numbers and ask you to call and get together with them that very same day or evening. They're not looking for a long-term relationship, they're just looking for a quick lay. Besides you're not the kind of girl who's available at the spur of the moment. And if you are, you shouldn't be.

2. Men who ask for more photos. They're classic narcissistic perfectionists and will drive you crazy. Two photos should be sufficient for anyone.

3. Men who don't ask for your number after two or three emails—especially the ones who want to get into deep, dark, lengthy conversations online. Who has time for that?

4. Men who have bad photos that don't appeal to you. Don't tell yourself you'll eventually get back to them after you've gone through your first picks. They're not ever going to look any better to you.

5. The man who corrects your grammar and/or edits

your profile. He is the classic criticizer, and will destroy you if you get into a relationship with him.

Take a little time, but not too much time, to get to know your potentials online first. Many people, myself included, don't like to write much. I'm much better over the phone and in person, and I know a lot of busy men who feel the same way. I don't care if a man makes a lot of typos, because I make a lot of them myself. Lisa, on the other hand, is a great lover of the written word (hence the writing of this book), and would give a man extra points if his messages and profile were well composed and free of grammatical errors. She ended up meeting her husband on JDate and knew she was going to love him before they even met in person because he wrote her free verse! But most of us don't have the patience for poetry and don't have time to mess around on the web for weeks before we meet face-to-face. I say if a guy hasn't arranged a date after two initial emails, he's not serious about looking for a wife, he's looking for an email buddy. Cut him off. He's too slow to be taken seriously.

When you do make a date to meet him, remember, **coffee is cheap, drinks are an audition, lunch is an interview, but dinner means business—the business of romance.** He's qualifying you like you're qualifying him. The fact that he'll spend money on you indicates that he's serious. All my boyfriends bought me dinner on the first date. A twenty-minute coffee date isn't even worth the time it takes to get out of bed and put on makeup. Since a coffee date is an audition, you can bet another girl will have been there before you, and another will step in twenty minutes later. Who wants to be subjected to that? If he's really interested in a relationship with you, he'll ask you out to dinner and pay.

Some men will argue and say, "I don't even know if I'm physically attracted to her! Why should I waste money on a meal until I find out?" That guy is not on the hunt for marriage. The guy who wants to get married wants to spend that money on you. The marriage-minded man is on a mission, he's reading these profiles, and is wise. He's exhausted by dating and just wants to find his match and get off the market. He needs one on one, quality time with you to figure out if you're The One. A decent guy will be content to spend a couple of hours with an attractive, happy woman, even if there's no chemistry. I've made some of my best male friends on internet dates—we weren't physically attracted to each other, but we liked each other's company so much we continued as friends, and, better yet as far as I'm concerned, as business associates.

Caution: The good thing about searching for your perfect match online is that you can get a plethora of information on him. The bad thing is that you can get a plethora of information on him. For example, while it's great to find out his hobbies, assets, and interests, many singles' sites allow you to get information that can drive you absolutely nuts! How many of us can resist the urge to log on and discern when he was last on the site, how much time he spent there, and whether or not he's online at that very moment? My advice is to keep yourself from checking him out as much as possible—after all, maybe he's logged on only to check and see if you're logged on, and you're only logged on to see if he's logged on, and you both think you're logged on to check out other people—for God's sake, it's a vicious circle you don't want to get caught in! Try logging on only in stealth mode, which many websites also allow. It will make the whole online process a lot more fun, discreet, and productive for you.

Another big problem with searching for your true love online is that there are so many ways to be deceitful. You really don't know anything about these guys, only what they choose to reveal, and no one is screening. They could have restraining orders against them, be seven years behind on their child support payments, or be convicted felons out on parole. That's why it's very important, until you get to know them better, to NEVER give out your home address. Don't allow them to come and pick you up for the first date. And don't give them your home phone number—did you know that anyone can google a home phone number and, if it's listed, the name and address associated with the number will pop up? Try it if you don't believe me. It's much better to give out your cell phone number.

When it comes time to meet face-to-face, make sure the venue is a restaurant or other well-lit public place. Check in with a girlfriend before you go. Tell her where you'll be and what time you're planning to arrive. Arrange to have her call you if you haven't already phoned her within an hour or two, and if she doesn't hear from you, she should come looking for you. This may sound paranoid, but you can never be too careful. And while we're on the subject, whatever you do, DO

NOT go back to his place afterward, no matter how trustworthy he seems. A classic case of bad judgment was written about in the newspaper recently. A girl met a man on a well-known, upscale dating site, they met at a restaurant, she went back to his place, and he allegedly raped her. This is what happens when a woman loses her mind after two drinks or more and feels connected to a guy simply because she relaxed on their date.

On that note, you would never drink too much in a business situation, so don't do it on a date. Even if he says he has something in his house you're just dying to see, whether it's a Picasso, a puppy, or a pool, save the viewing for a later date when you know more about him. Even the nicest, safest guys will get the message that you're ready to roll if you go back to their place too soon.

Internet dating can also become addictive. It can rule your life if you're not careful, and make your forget there are other ways to meet men. Both men and women find themselves joining several different sites and checking their email every five minutes. They race home after a date to see if anyone new has contacted them and keep twenty to thirty correspondences going at the same time. They waste massive amounts of time instant messaging and chatting, and at the same time they're searching other people's profiles. They stay up late, spending hours online, trying to find someone new, or someone they might have overlooked before. My advice is to not spend more than an hour a day, preferably less, on online dating and as I've mentioned before, make it only one third of your search.

Personal Contacts

Meeting your potential mate through someone who already knows him is hands down the safest and most efficient way to make your own match. You know where he lives, you know where he works, you have at least one personal recommendation, and you can have your big brother hunt him down and kick his ass if he's mean to you. Just kidding . . . sort of. But he will be more inclined to be on his best behavior if he knows you'll be reporting back to the mutual friend or matchmaker who introduced you. Why not have someone you know and trust do the screening for you? It can save you a great deal of time, money, and heartache.

You can approach your friends, family members, or business associates about any interesting singles they know who are looking for a committed relationship. People are more receptive to this than you might think—this is a good way for them to do a great favor for two people at once. Your married friends can be especially good resources, because A: They're not in competition with you, and B: They're all about helping you share the joy (or misery), they're experiencing as a couple. You can always flatter them by saying something like, "Your husband is such a great guy, does he have any available brothers or friends?" This also opens up the possibility of meeting that guy on a double date with your friends, or at a party where there are other people around to reduce the pressure.

Also, don't be afraid to ask people you strike up random conversations with for dating referrals. How many times have you been in a nail salon, or on a plane, and some sweet little old lady seated next to you said, "You seem like a charming girl. I have a grandson . . ." Or an attractive married man says, "Hey, I know a great single guy who lives near you . . ." This happens all the time. And when it does, I want you to be ready with Bio Cards.

Bio Cards: Don't Go Out Without Them

The Bio Card is the size of a postcard. On one side you have that stunning photo you had taken for your internet profile. On the flip side, you have your personal information, possibly the bio you wrote for the dating site, where you went to school, where you grew up, and a cell phone number, but never your address. Bio Cards may sound pushy and desperate to some people, but hear me out. Men are **visually** oriented. They are ten times more likely to call you if they see your picture and read a little bit about you, than if their aunt hands them a business card and says "Call this girl, she's got a sweet spirit." Chances are he'll put the business card in his pocket and forget about it, but a postcard-size bio and picture will give him something to fantasize about. I know this from personal experience. I've seen men get on their cell phones and dial the number immediately when I give them a female club member's Bio Card with a sexy picture on it. But the same guy will "accidentally" forget the plain business card and leave it behind on the table. Why do you think so many real estate agents put their photos on their cards? People respond quicker and better to a happy face.

I'm not recommending that you hand out your Bio Cards

on a street corner or do a mass mailing. I'm just saying you should carry some around in your purse and always be prepared. **In order to scout good boys, you have to be a good Boy Scout.**

Pay It Forward

You might have already tried asking your girlfriends to introduce you to their single guy friends, and been met with lame excuses like, "Gee, I don't really know anybody . . ." or, "All my friends are married." Don't let them get away with that! Women can be so catty and competitive! We need to start looking at each other as sisters, not as competition. Anyway, a great way to disarm your single friends and convince them to introduce you to your potential perfect match is to "pay it forward." This involves first offering to introduce your friends to the eligible people in your circle. If you're single, chances are you know many others who are in the same boat. Why not get them together? You'll probably find them very grateful and willing to return the favor.

As a matter of fact, I found my last boyfriend through someone offering to pay it forward for me. When you're a professional matchmaker, it's hard to look at the single men you meet as potential husbands for yourself—you get in the habit of looking at them as potential clients or matches for someone else. So one day I got a phone call from a woman I'll call Andrea, who wanted to come to work for me as a matchmaker for the Millionaire's Club. Now, matchmaking is an art, refined over the years, and just because you think you're good at lining people up doesn't necessarily mean you're good at helping people find their other half. Andrea was a professional and knew she'd need to prove herself, so she said to me, "Why don't you let me show you what I can do by lining you up?" Wow! I was impressed! No one offers to make a match for the matchmaker! "It's a deal," I told her.

The first guy turned out to be one of the loves of my life, and we were very happily ensconced in a committed, monogamous relationship for a long time. Think of paying it forward as investing in a sort of Dating 401(k). You're saving up favors that you'll be able to tap into at the right time, and best of all, there are no penalties for early withdrawal.

Matchmaker, Matchmaker, Make Me a Match

While we're on the subject of professional matchmakers, let me put in a word for them. This is certainly not just to build my own business, but because I'm so intimately involved with the profession, I know just how well it can work for you. Hiring a private matchmaker may sound intimidating and expensive, but I see it as a smart and efficient way to invest in your future, especially if you're over forty, when your choices have diminished. Consider this: if you're willing to spend money on the designer bag, the nice car, the nice furnishings for your home, the fun vacations, and the other things you really want, why not be willing to spend money on the man and the future you really want?

There are plenty of great personal matchmaking services in the US. The nice thing about them is that they will do the work FOR you. On the internet, you have to work for yourself. Your matchmaker will have screened the men beforehand, and won't waste your time with inappropriate guys. He or she will pitch you to your potential date, so you don't have to feel awkward pitching yourself. A good matchmaker will show you photos of the men and give you unlimited dating throughout your membership. And, best of all, your match-maker will handle rejection for you, sparing you the humilia-tion of hearing it straight from the horse's mouth. You'll also get helpful feedback from the matchmaker, so you can learn from your experience and mistakes, rather than constantly wondering if it went wrong because of some random thing you said or did.

Don't confuse a dating service with a personal match-making service. Dating services like Great Expectations pres-ent you to other singles who have joined the service, but they don't guarantee you dates. They can give you the opportunity to meet other eligibles, but a matchmaker will be personally proactive in finding you The One.

Not all professional matchmakers are created equal, of course. Do a Google search on the matchmakers, and confirm that they haven't received any negative press lately and are not the objects of any lawsuits. Find out how long they've been in business—preferably for a number of years. A lot of matchmakers, myself included, get their starts at dating ser-vices and then move on. Ask detailed questions, such as how many clients they have who would be appropriate for you to date, and ask to see photos and profiles. A good matchmaker will not only let you see her database of men, but she'll go outside of her database and recruit for you. The best mem-berships include unlimited dating for a year, a discount in your second year, and the opportunity to freeze your membership for a limited amount of time—two months maybe—while you try out someone you think you might want to become exclusive with. It's very important to get at least three references from people in your own age group. Make sure you call those references.

Don't be upset if the matchmaker doesn't take credit cards. As horrified as I am to tell you this, when I worked at Great Expectations, many people would meet their first date and get married. Because they were within their thirty-day billing cycle, they would dispute the charge on their cards and get their money back—the credit card companies always take the cardholder's side. Good matchmakers know this and will often charge you money up front, accepting cash or checks. Your membership will not usually activate until your check or money order has cleared. A really good matchmaker (like me) will get you on a date within twenty-four hours of your check clearing. If your matchmaker tells you it's taking weeks to process your info, she doesn't have anyone for you and is scrambling to find someone. This is the danger zone.

Oftentimes, those who are disgruntled about matchmakers are not the ones who didn't get serviced. The complainers are usually the ones who were given good match candidates, but the candidates didn't like them. Please remember, matchmakers can't make anyone fall in love with you. As long as she's giving you qualified candidates, she's no different from a headhunter in business. The headhunter can get you the interview, but she can't get you the job.

I'm more than happy to provide the best service for my

paying clients, because I'm so good at what I do. The shortest membership my clients can purchase is one year, but it seldom takes them more than two months to become involved in a serious, monogamous relationship unless they're a serial dater and they don't really want a relationship—the George Clooney types. There are those who use my service for years, always wanting someone new.

I'm not just trying to drum up business for myself here. To be honest, my fees are higher than the average Joe or Jane wants to pay, and you'd be surprised by how some of the wealthiest men in the country try to finagle a better price. A paid membership in the Millionaire's Club runs from $25,000 to $150,000 per year depending on what type of services the client desires. If the Millionaire's Club can't service you, we'll refer you to an affiliated program that we have screened in advance. Remember, we are a boutique agency and not for everyone. However, every woman who reads this book can register for free in our database. If we have a potential date for you, we will contact you once you register online at MillionairesClub123.com. Women join the Millionaire's Club for free, unless they pay my fee for active recruiting. This is the millionairess membership. Non-millionaire men may also join the club for free, if they want to put their names, profiles, and photos in my database and wait for a woman or gay man to pick them. No non-paying member is guaranteed a date.

If you want a professional to get out and actively search for you, it's definitely worth the investment to pay for them to do so, in my service or others that might better fit into your price range. To give you an idea of fees, on the low end, a professional matchmaker will charge you around $5,000 for a year; the average is about $10,000 per year, unless there are additional services. That's a lot less than you'd pay a personal publicist, and a matchmaker gives you the same type of service, except you're being publicized to a handpicked demographic that will work best for you.

But if you're just not willing to spend that much on a matchmaker, consider taking out an ad on a popular website like Craigslist, to find someone to introduce you to people at parties, openings, and other social events. Offer to pay this person by the hour or by the event. Social butterfly types who are in need of a little extra cash love to do this. Or find someone with a huge circle of friends and offer to pay them by the date they line up for you. There are many socialites out there who wouldn't mind being paid for the favors they usually do for free. This would have been my next step if I hadn't found my last boyfriend. I'd already tried online dating and met most of my friends' single connections. Since I've made it an unwavering policy never to date any of my clients, I thought it might help to pay someone to fish in other ponds for me.

Some specialty matchmakers will give you dates if you send them your leftover men. For example, back in my early dating days, I knew a local matchmaker who needed Jewish men for her Jewish women. Every Jewish guy who I came across and didn't want to date, I referred to her, and she'd give me a date with one of the men she represented. Matchmakers need new product daily. They're constantly looking to refresh their databases. If you offer them the type of men or women they need, they will often reward you with a date. It's much easier for a matchmaker to reward you with another man than to pay you with cash. And if you're the type of social butterfly who goes to events and meets people, you can make a good living recruiting for these services. They're always hiring.

And don't overlook another great matchmaking resource that is available to you for free. If you're religious, approach your pastor, rabbi, priest, etc., to help you find a mate who shares your faith. The best-kept secret is the rabbi's or pastor's wife. They are constantly looking to marry off members of their flocks. They also know everyone. Suck up, buy her a spa treatment, and that will get you noticed in the pews. My rabbi's wife sent me a number of great people when I was looking for good Jewish girls for my clients.

Out and About

As much help as you get from other people and from internet dating services, know that you'll have to do at least a third of your matchmaking work on your own. You need to be proactive and make the effort yourself, even if it involves moving outside your comfort zone and boldly going where you've never gone before. Start frequenting the places where single men gather—put yourself smack dab in the middle of their radar. You must go to them, because, honey, they're not going to come to you, no matter what you hear about the pizza guy appearing at your door with a steaming hot pepperoni and a ring. That only happens in porn movies. You have a much better chance of meeting a straight single guy at a ball game or a sports bar than you do at the nail salon or shopping at Victoria's Secret, and you'll never meet anybody sitting at home on your duff. I'm just saying . . .

Before I give you a list of happy hunting grounds, it is imperative that you know the following, unequivocal fact about your search: **those who travel in packs do not attract.** You must be willing to visit these places alone. I cannot over-stress the importance of this. You may want to take your homegirls along for moral support, but a pack of females is intimidating to these poor guys. Think of a scared bunny try-ing to approach a pack of wolves. If some guy has the balls to approach a group of women, he faces potential rejection and derision from not one, but a whole group of vicious females.

Besides, unless you're a smoking hot 12 on a scale of 1–10, chances are that someone in your girl group is going to be more attractive than you are, and she'll get all the best mas-culine attention, while all you can hope for is her leftovers. The Denise Richards types will move right in and steal your man before you can even say hi. And there's always the one girl in the group who calls dibs on a guy before you even see him, thus robbing you of the opportunity to flirt with him according to Girl Code. Why bother with any of those com-plications? Your time is much better spent going out alone.

While doing some activities alone may be easy for you to consider, I know that the prospect of going out alone might make you uncomfortable. That's why I have a number of tricks to help make it easier and more enjoyable for you. Identify an upscale restaurant or hotel in your area that has a congenial bar or lounge area. A place that has a happy hour with food is good—men LOVE food, and they hate to eat alone. Go there right after work, before it gets too crowded, and start chatting up the bartender. If you can get out of work early, a good time to go is about 4:30 PM. The place will be empty, and you'll get your pick of the perfect bar seat. Plus, the bartender will be setting up, and you'll have someone to chat with. Tip him or her well, and inquire about the vibe of the place. That way, when the single men arrive, you'll already have an ally who will be eager to introduce you to eligible men. Why? If he introduces you to a heavy hitter, the heavy hitter will pay for his drinks, your drinks, maybe even dinner, and the bartender will get a bigger tip. Another reason he'll do this is that if the potential guy is a bar hopper and he doesn't see any female action, he will move on to the next bar, and the bartender loses a good customer.

Take along a copy of a gender-neutral bestseller, like *Eat, Pray, Love*—no chick lit. Books are great conversation starters. Or if you go to a hotel like the Four Seasons, they'll offer you reading material when you're sitting in the lounge alone. Accept it and enjoy it, but don't be so intent on your reading material that a man will feel awkward coming between you and your op-ed piece.

Still feeling silly being there by yourself? Frequently glance at your watch, then at the door, as if you're waiting for someone to meet you. Actually, you are, so this is not deceptive or dishonest. You're waiting for Mr. Right, and if anyone asks, you can honestly tell them, "I'm supposed to meet someone here, but I'm not sure if he's going to make it." It can be your own little private joke.

The Five-Second Flirt

This is a sure man-catching technique that's been passed down in our family for generations. It works every time. A great time to try it is when you already have a date, and I'll tell you why: women feel the most content when they're getting plenty of attention from men—they're no longer in heat. If you already have a date, you feel more confident, even if that date is just with a friend. Because your vibration is content and confident, you'll send off a very attractive signal to the opposite sex.

There you are, sitting at the bar waiting for your date to arrive, you're smiling, smelling good, and feeling sexy. There will probably be a lot of single men around you (men who are not wearing wedding rings). Notice the one guy in the room who you'd really like to meet, and make sure he's not with another woman. Catch his eye and hold his gaze for five full seconds, while giving him your most radiant smile. Then flip your hair and turn away. This might seem awkward, but you can start by practicing in the mirror. If you still feel terrified, practice this on men you don't find attractive—you have nothing to lose since there's no risk.

When you give a man the five second flirt he will either walk over to you to start a conversation, or he won't. If he comes over to you and offers to buy or refresh your drink, you might have a potential mate on your hands. If he doesn't offer to do this after ten minutes of chatting, he's an inconsiderate narcissist. Move on.

But what if he never comes over to you after the five second flirt? What's that about? There are four reasons for this:

1. He's married or in a relationship.
2. He's playing on the other team (he's gay).
3. You're not his type. You're blonde, and he goes for brunettes; there's nothing you can do about that. Forget about him.
4. He's a Passive Aggressive and wants you to chase him. If you do talk to him, he'll end up giving you his business card and asking *you* to call *him*. He's not worth your time.

Where Your Future Husband Will Find You

And now, the part you've been waiting for. Here's a list of manly-man places where you can test these tactics and see just how well they work:

SPORTS BARS: Most men don't take dates to sports bars, but hang with their buddies to watch their favorite teams play on the big screen. If you go there alone and know the score and a little bit about the teams playing, you will get more attention than you ever believed possible.

My friend Lily decided she was going to go out by herself to the most exclusive sports bar in LA, known as The Parlor. She was a big Lakers fan, and wanted to make the most of watching the NBA playoffs. She made a great move when she walked in. The place was swarming with men, and she walked right up to the hostess and asked who owned the joint. Turns out it belonged to the hottest guy in the place, a supersexy guy named Silas, who you might recognize from reality TV. He'd noticed Lily right away, but already had a girlfriend, so before you could say "Go Kobe," he was introducing her to all his buddies at the bar. He got her a stool and a turkey burger, and suddenly she was in the club. The first time she went to the sports bar she made guy friends. The second time she made a girlfriend who introduced her to still more guys. The third time she started talking to one of the guys she'd met on a previous visit, and he ended up becoming her boyfriend. So by going to the sports bar alone, she found a new best girl friend, a local hangout where everybody knows her name, and a boyfriend too!

PROFESSIONAL SPORTING EVENTS: Baseball, basketball, football, soccer, hockey, you name it, men outnumber women by at least ten to one at these events. Basketball and hockey games are the most expensive—that's where you'll find the real heavy hitters. If you're looking for a wealthy guy but can't afford the tickets to sit in the VIP section, buy nosebleed tickets, and get your snacks during halftime and at quarter breaks at the concession stands closest to the premier seats. If you're attractively dressed, the ushers won't question you when you try to enter these exclusive areas, and if they do, you can just say, "My boyfriend has our tickets inside, I had to leave because the ladies' rooms here were just too crowded." If you have an American Express Platinum Card, you'll be allowed access to VIP areas in most stadiums in the US during the regular season.

STEAK HOUSES: When they get together for a night out with the boys, do you think they're going to hit a salad buffet? Real men eat meat. Many enjoy a good steak and a martini. Most of these restaurants have a nice lounge or bar area. It's a great place to hit during happy hour, when they're waiting for their guy friends to arrive. My favorite is The Palm, which is an extremely upscale national chain. But there are plenty of others to choose from like Morton's or Ruth's Chris.

DRIVING RANGES: Avid golfers like to hit the driving range on their way home from work and on weekends to take their frustrations out on the ball. Don't worry if you're not that good. Men love to coach you, and are flattered when you make positive comments about their swing and ask them for tips. If you want to make the effort to take lessons and develop a decent game and golf-course etiquette, golfers will take notice and invite you to go 18 with them.

TENNIS CLUBS: Join one. Community clubs aren't that expensive, it's a fabulous way to keep in shape, and who knows who they'll pair you with in the next tournament? Tennis tournaments are one of the best-kept secrets in town, as they often last a week or two and include a fairly upscale crowd.

MOVIE THEATERS: You won't find a guy when you're sitting alone in the dark, silly. It's the lines outside of action flicks, war movies, westerns, or superhero films where you're likely to meet your match. I can't tell you how many conversations I've struck up in theater lines in New York that eventually led to dates. People are often afraid to go to movies by themselves, but if you think about it, you're in the dark for two hours and you can't talk anyway, so what have you got to lose?

CLASSES: A great way to meet men who have similar interests as you is by taking continuing education classes. If you're movie minded, find men who are too through film courses at your local college, which often include a screening, a dinner, and a lecture by the filmmaker. NYU and the New School in the New York area are known for this.

SALSA AND COUNTRY DANCE CLUBS: The advantage to these types of dancing, as opposed to others, is that both country and Latin dances must be done with a partner. Those yummy Latino men and cowboys can be *muy sabroso*! Many of these clubs have nights where there's a dinner and a dance lesson before the real dancing begins, so take advantage of those. Not only are they great places to meet men, but they are so much fun. Because of the success of *Dancing with the Stars*, dance schools like Arthur Murray are becoming more popular, and they often pair you up with a potential dance partner for life. Real men do dance.

PREPARED FOOD AISLE AT THE SUPERMARKET: Forget the produce aisle or the meat counter, most men these days don't want to take the time to cook and prefer to pick up something ready-made. The best time to hit the grocery store is right after work on weekdays. On Saturdays and Sundays married men usually shop with their wives. Your local neighborhood market, rather than a big supermarket, can be a great place to meet guys. At these smaller stores, men are more likely to establish relationships with the butcher, who you can ask for information about the men you're eager to meet. If you're a vegan and want to go the health route, there's no better place than Whole Foods. Another place to find single men is at Costco on the weekends, lingering over the free sample tables when they come to pick up their bulk toilet paper and paper towels.

SUSHI BAR: This is the one place men will sit down and eat alone. Don't ask for a table. Sidle up to the bar, make friends with the sushi chef, and just see who plops down on the stool next to you. When I was living in New York, this was my staple after working out at the gym. I would meet more men at the sushi bar, many of them coming from the gym as well, and they were as hungry and lonely as I was. The sushi bar gives you the opportunity to talk and get to know each other. You know he's a real keeper when he pays for your dinner.

AUTO AND BOAT SHOWS: This is a man-meeting Mecca— every guy's wet dream. A girl who shares an interest in cars or boats is every straight man's fantasy. Get the convention center schedule and mark off these events. The best days to go are the first and last days of the show. The first day gets all the press, and there are the most giveaways. Men love their freebie key chains. On the last day they know that they are more likely to get deals. It's best to go on a weekend rather than during the week, although on a weekday you'll find the wealthy men who don't have to go to work. Motorcycle shows are good too.

INDUSTRY EVENTS: Figure out what industry rules your town, and show up at conferences, lectures, and promotional events. In LA it's the entertainment industry. In New York it's finance. In Detroit it's the auto industry. In Washington it's politics. In Seattle it's the computer industry. In Silicon Valley it's high tech. You get the drift. If you're wondering how to get into an event you're not connected to, google the trade show and you'll find a list of events, receptions, and lectures that are open to the general public. You might want to contact the organization itself to get access. Since these particular organizations need new members, they often welcome beautiful girls to attend their cocktail parties. It keeps members happy and brings in new ones. Real estate events throw the best, most lavish cocktail parties of all, since they're known for seducing their buyers with alcohol before they purchase a condo or home. My single girlfriends and I used to go to those in Florida all the time (but not together).

CIGAR BARS: These are becoming increasingly popular among men across the country. Most women can't stand the smell of cigars, but if you're one of the lucky women who can, you will have your pick of the myriad men in these locations. Places like the Grand Havana Room in Los Angeles attract celebrities. It's a members-only establishment, but they often have cocktail parties to attract new members. All you have to do is call to find out about new-member events.

UPSCALE CAR DEALERSHIPS: No, you don't hang out there, but dealerships like Mercedes and BMW throw cocktail parties for new owners, or to present a special new model to their longtime customers. If you buy one of these luxury cars, you're automatically on the invite list, but if you're not you can express interest in buying one and ask them to put you on it. Believe it or not, your sales rep can also introduce you to eligible men. He knows exactly what the guys are buying, what they're interested in, practically what color of underwear they're wearing. Car dealers to men are like hairdressers to women. Make friends with one, offer to send him referrals in exchange for matches, and he will lick your feet.

WINE TASTINGS: For some reason there are usually more men than women at these events. You can find out about wine tastings at your local wine store, some posh food markets, and occasionally restaurants sponsor them as well. Google Wine Brats in your area—it's a singles' wine group. And since that has become famous, more singles' wine groups have been popping up all over the country. They often attract an Ivy League, upper echelon male, and sometimes metrosexuals, but at least they're single.

POLITICAL SUPPORT GROUPS: Dynamic, committed men tend to be politically active, and the single ones have more time for this sort of thing. Volunteer for a group, and there you'll find men who share your passions. Get involved during an election or right after, when the new administration is looking for fresh meat. You'll find a lot of hopefuls.

MARATHONS: It seems there's some sort of a "run for fun" or 10K fund-raiser going on in every city, every weekend. Not only do you stand a great chance of meeting an interesting man while training, but remember that the endorphin rush will make you glow and keep you fit. He'll be impressed by your stamina and commitment to running the good race.

OUTDOOR SPORTING EVENTS: Polo and golf tournaments, horse races, NASCAR and other auto races are exceptional places to meet single, heterosexual men. Men usually attend these events with the guys, rather than dates.

SPECIAL INTEREST GROUPS: You're sure to find many eligible men doing manly activities like hiking, sailing, fishing, flying, kayaking, and beach cleanups. Sierra Club is a really great place to meet eco-friendly, green men. In California we actually have green speed dating (or "carbon neutral love") and your price of admission goes straight toward saving the environment.

SKI RESORTS: The male-female odds are in your favor at all ski resorts, and you get the added benefit of having the singles and couples presorted for you in the lift lines. I've seen men duck the ropes to change lift lines and leave their buddies stranded when an attractive girl calls, "single!" The most and best resorts for singles are in Colorado, (metrosexuals in Aspen, family guys in Vail) but don't rule out Windsor in Canada—those Canadians snatch the women up fast. My personal favorite is Jackson Hole, where there are plenty of cowboys and oil millionaires.

DOG PARKS: A single guy who takes good care of his dog is usually one who is more open to responsibility and commitment. Besides, most have a "love my dog, love me" attitude. If you can win over the man's best friend, you can win over the man. Dog guys are usually more masculine, while cat guys lean more toward the metrosexual side.

HOBBY AND FAN CONVENTIONS: Don't rule out techno nerds from the electronics show, or the sci-fi or comics guy. Silicon Valley–type guys hang in groups, or in pods, as I like to call them, like dolphins or whales. There are always about twelve in a group together, and they have no fear. When they see anything with tits, they jump. Pretend like you don't know how to play a video game, and they're all over you. Remember, these guys are the future zillionaires. They can fix anything—your computer, your toaster, your car. That, to me, is a real turn on. If you think Mr. Star Wars is the neighborhood nerd, think again. All guys love *Star Trek*, from the original to the next generations. They come in all varieties and sizes and they are the future. Take Mr. Comic-Con. He might be blogging about his favorite superhero, but he's a romantic at heart, because every superhero saves the damsel in distress. A favorite friend of mine is an übercollector, one of the biggest guys in the memorabilia business, and trust me, he is no nerd. He might be an ex-hippy, but he's also a sexy stud, and he's made a fortune from auctioning music and movie memorabilia. That's the kind of guy you could stumble across at a hobby or fan convention.

FOOD, WINE, AND MUSIC FESTIVALS: Where there's a festival, there's usually good eats, and, as I've mentioned before, men love food. They also love their favorite bands. Put them all together, and you have one very happy, receptive mass of masculinity, not to mention one of my favorite places to be. And, trust me, most groups of guys who go to concerts together would much rather be with a woman. Nighttime is for romance, after all.

ELECTRONICS STORES: I get so bored at these stores my eyes glaze over, until I notice the huge numbers of men wandering the aisles. Whether it's Circuit City, Best Buy, or your favorite local big-screen TV store, men will be absolutely thrilled to give you advice on a purchase. As television goes digital, you'll have more questions to ask than ever. Do not ask the idiot, seventh-grade educated Best Buy boy when you're looking for an electronics device. Ask the handsome guy who has a ton of electronic gadgets in his basket. He will help you, and maybe you'll score a date. That happened to me just months ago. I was in a store trying to decide whether to switch to an iPhone from a BlackBerry, and a really handsome guy walked up to me and started advising me, telling me that he loved my show. He then asked for my phone number, and I reluctantly had to tell him I had a boyfriend. Boy, is some other lucky girl going to score with him!

BOWLING ALLIES AND AMUSEMENT ARCADES: The low-rent places are rapidly disappearing from the landscape and are being replaced by clean, upscale, well-lit venues like Boomers! and Dave & Buster's. These are high-end arcade chains that have every amusement you could imagine, even karaoke and dinner. My favorite is virtual reality skiing. Be sure to hang out by the batting cages, shooting, golf, and driving games—that's where the masculine guys are. Upscale bowling allies have also come into vogue. They're fun, chic, and many have theme nights a few times a week that can be fun. And bowling leagues have become hip again.

SCUBA DIVING: The men you dive with will be sweeter than molasses. They will take your hand and help you every step of the way, because they know that women are often frightened underwater, and they want to protect you. It's easy to do an intro dive at a local resort, but to get certification requires a class where you'll see guys week after week and build a relationship. I've heard of many girls meeting their boyfriends in scuba class, where even the instructors are good looking—they're in great shape from schlepping gear, have no fear, and great tans. If you're in swimsuit shape, what could be better than showing a lot of skin while hanging out for several hours on a boat or underwater with a bunch of athletic guys? And if scuba's not your thing, you can still surround yourself with half-naked, chiseled men if you go Jet Skiing, water-skiing, windsurfing, parasailing, or surfing.

SINGLES' VACATIONS: Men especially love the action adventure trips that involve active sports like biking, hiking, river rafting, climbing, skiing, deep-sea fishing, sailing, or horseback riding. Men love horses. You can find these types of vacations if you google them, but you can also check the back of *Men's Health* or *Men's Fitness* magazines. I've always wanted to go to Vancouver where you can kayak among orca whales, and swimming with the dolphins is a great way to meet a gorgeous marine biologist–type.

VEGAS, BABY!: Not only do men love to golf, gamble, and attend bachelor parties here, but many are drawn to the big conventions like the Consumer Electronics Show (CES), the National Association of Broadcasters (NAB) convention, and ShoWest, for the film industry. Granted, many of the men here are out-of-towners, but then again, so are you, and if you plan your vacation right, you just might meet someone from your neck of the woods. Learn how to play poker before you go—they don't call it Texas Hold'em for nothing! A great place to go is the Hard Rock Hotel and Casino where the largest amount of single men congregate nightly because they love to listen to rock music while they gamble. Also, the dealers love to see you win and get excited when you do, which is a nice touch. No other casino does this. And the casino is in the round, so you can see all the action as it's happening live. It's easy to scan for your potential honey while sipping your mojito and winning at 21. If you're in bikini shape, the Hard Rock in the summer has what they call Rehab, but it has nothing to do with drug detox. It's an open pool party, set on a faux beach, complete with rock music and jumbo-size drinks. Make sure you get there early if you're not staying in the hotel, because lounges and cabanas are on a first come, first served basis. If you like the high rollers, head over to the Playboy Club at the Palms, which attracts a young but rich crowd. If you'd like a more mature big spender, the Wynn and the Bellagio are your best bets.

CHARITY EVENTS: The man you find at the research fund-raiser, the beach cleanup, the pet adoption, or the Big Brothers Big Sisters event, is the man with a good heart. If tickets to the charity event of your choice are too expensive, volunteer. You might be surprised to find out that a single man will attend these events alone or with his sister rather than waste $1,200 on a ticket for a woman he's not that into. Of all the places on the list, this one is the best. When I ran Great Expectations special events, the main place we looked for singles was in the charity circuit. American Cancer Society, Covenant House, the Jewish Federation, and the March of Dimes are just a few of the charities that have events for singles of all ages. Check the society section of your paper, or look up the charity online to find out about their yearly events. They have everything from picnics to date auctions to dog jogs.

Where the Boys Aren't

Some of these might come as a shock to you, because you've been told repeatedly that these are good places to meet men.

But considering the feedback I get from the women in the Millionaire's Club, as well as my own personal experience, don't expect to find a red-blooded, straight, eligible guy in the following places:

SPIRITUAL CLASSES AND WORKSHOPS: Very few men are working on metaphysical self-improvement, and if they are, they're usually looking within, not without. Leave them alone and let them contemplate in peace. They're usually trying to solve personal problems and are not ready for committed relationships. Very rarely will you find a single, successful, open-minded man who is not mentally twisted at one of these classes or workshops. If you want to go to these places for yourself, fine, but don't go to find love.

GYMS AND/OR FITNESS CENTERS: Yes, fit, heterosexual guys work out in gyms, but so do superhot heterosexual twenty-one-year-old women, and unless you're one of them, you're not going to stand a chance at a gym. In theory they're great places to get your endorphins flowing to make you feel sexy. However, the gym is also the number one place for the serial dater to hang. He's overly obsessed with keeping fit and has probably slept with every female at the gym. And if you think you're going to date your trainer, think again. We all know somebody who has been through the trainer experience, and it's a time waster.

HOT BARS AND CLUBS: Men usually go there to score for a night, not to find their life partners. That's because bars today attract alcoholics. Also, if you go to clubs, you can't hear yourself speak, the techno music will give you a headache, and unless you're blonde, you're in trouble; brunettes do not stand out in the dark.

CRUISE SHIPS: Single, straight men do not go on cruises with their buddies, or alone. It's something they do with a wife, a girlfriend, or their mother for her birthday.

STARBUCKS, OR THE LOCAL COFFEEHOUSE: If a guy is hanging out there, especially with his computer, he probably doesn't have an office to work in, or, worse yet, he's unemployed or poor. In any case, he ain't husband material.

SALONS: Most straight men spend as little time as possible here—they want to get in and get out without being noticed. And if they're getting a mani or a pedi, it's because they're gay or their wives or girlfriends dragged them in.

BRUNCH BUFFETS: This is definitely a date or girlie-girl venue—just one more activity that groups of straight, single men do not attend together. There is one exception, though. If you're staying in a luxury hotel or resort, groups of men on business trips will brunch together. It can be a pretty tasty buffet.

FROZEN YOGURT SHOPS: When was the last time you heard a manly man say, "Hey guys, let's go get smoothies!" When straight guys go out for treats, it usually involves alcohol, but an alternative could be Baskin-Robbins or Cold Stone Creamery, especially in the summer.

LAUNDROMATS: Sure, we see plenty of commercials where hot guys and girls get together during the rinse cycle. But watching each other sort granny panties and threadbare boxer shorts is really not a great place to start. Besides, doesn't he have better things to do than hang out in a Laundromat? Successful men will have their clothes laundered by a service, or throw them in their own washing machines.

Now that you know where to go and where not to go to be surrounded by hundreds of eligible men, your biggest problem is going to be deciding which one to grace with your attention. You don't want to waste your time with vapid pretty boys, bigger, better dealers, or lazy commitmentphobes. So many choices, so little time! Next up: how to Qualify the Buyer. Here I'll show you how to only choose the men who will make the best match for you. You're going to love me for this.

STEP FOUR

Qualifying the Buyer

Finding the right guy is like finding the perfect pair of shoes. You want to find the perfect pair that is gorgeous, sexy, fits just right, and will stand the test of time. You want to be able to stand and walk in them for blocks and still be comfortable. But what do most of us do when we go shoe shopping? We buy a pair that's on sale that looks expensive and maybe pinches just a little, but we don't care because they're gorgeous. We take them home, wear them a few times, then realize we have to relegate them to the back of the closet because the more we wear them, the worse they hurt.

In husband shopping, as in shoe shopping, in order to keep from making the same mistake again and again, you need to learn not to buy the first one you see just because it has a great label. Remember that some of the best shoes are found in little, out-of-the-way shops no one knows about. Just because they're popular doesn't mean they're comfortable. You need to take your time shopping and ask yourself, are these shoes really worth the expensive price tag? Will they be a classic staple or a passing fad? Will they take you from funerals to weddings to business functions, or will you wear them for ten minutes, then kick them off at the party? In order to find that perfect pair of shoes, you have to decide exactly what you want, then go out there and find it. They are not going to jump off the shelf and run up to you.

So many girls stand on the sidelines, passively waiting to be picked. Wrong tactic! My mom used to say to me, "A good woman will signal a man, then let him come to her." Remember, you're not in a hurry (at least you shouldn't be). You should take your time to prequalify all prospective candidates, and wait until the perfect husband comes along. After all, you want your marriage to last a lifetime, don't you?

I used to be in a big hurry. My mother's best friend told me that if I didn't meet my husband in college, that was it. All bets were off, and I'd be stuck a spinster for the rest of my life. When I was still single at my college graduation, I thought, "Oh my gosh! Lights out! I'm done! Washed up at twenty-two!" Obviously this woman was bat-ass crazy, because the median age for marriage today is twenty-nine. If you don't believe me, read the wedding announcements in your local paper. How many girls do you see who are getting married at twenty-one or twenty-two? That might have been common in the '50s, but not today. And for you girls over forty, don't fret. My perfect match didn't come along in my twenties when I was effortlessly skinny and looked my best. He didn't come along in my thirties when I was involved in a great career and still had some good childbearing years left. I finally found what I believe is my perfect match when I was forty-two. My writing partner, Lisa, found hers at forty-six. But we didn't put our lives on hold until our true loves showed up. We traveled, we made money, we invested, we did charity work—I can tell you it's worth the wait. It may happen later in life, but he will come, I promise you. My hand to God.

Lots of celebrities get married for the first time over forty. Let's take a look at the tape on that: Desperate Housewife Marcia Cross was over forty when she married her over-forty husband, and she had babies at age forty-six. Julianna Margulies married a successful lawyer from New York when she was over forty-two. Nancy Grace married a friend of a friend in her late forties, then had twins. These women were smart and didn't give into the Hollywood pressure of buying too early. Like real estate agents, they took time to qualify their buyers.

Realtors are encouraged to qualify potential home-buying clients to find out if they're truly in a position to buy or just looking around. What they determine makes a huge difference in the amount of time they spend with a potential client. They'll ask questions like:

Is this your first purchase?
How long have you been looking?
Do you have good credit?
How much money can you qualify to borrow?
Do you know what features are absolutely essential?
Do you need to sell your current home before you buy a
    new one?
How soon do you want to be in your new home?

Will you be fixing it up?
Are you willing to redecorate?

Smart women assess the potential buyer as quickly as possible, not wasting any more time than is needed, before they get all wrapped up in someone who can't possibly afford what they have to offer. Parallel questions having to do with a potential match would be:

Is this your first marriage/long-term relationship?
How long have you been looking for your perfect honey?
Do you have enough money to support me in the way I've become accustomed?
Is there someone out there who will vouch for you?
What are the features you're looking for in a wife?
Do you have a solid foundation, as in a job and/or career? (there is a difference, you know)
Do you have good credit?
Are you a marriage-minded man, ready to pack his bags and move into commitment tomorrow, or are you still in looking mode?
Do you need to get rid of an ex or a backup girl before you commit?
Ideally, how soon would you like to be settled down in a monogamous relationship?

Of course, you don't ask these questions outright. When your date opens up and starts asking you qualifying questions, you can ping-pong right back and say, "I feel . . . and you?" If he doesn't open up, you can search the conversation for little tidbits of information. For example, a comment such as, "I've been living in this house for four years, ever since I got divorced," signals that his marriage is long gone and that he is certainly ready to move on.

If his answers to these questions don't mesh with yours, you need to throw him back and cast a new line. The most important thing of all to remember is YOU CAN'T CHANGE HIM! To push the fishing metaphor a little farther, you can't change a shark into a dolphin when it gets caught in your net. Most men are fairly straightforward about their relationship goals (except the real bastards). If they tell you they're not interested in settling down right now, believe them. In the beginning, men are not as guarded as women are. They usually tell you whatever pops into their heads— they have no filter. You need to listen carefully.

So many of us say to ourselves, "Well, he says he's not ready for marriage, but just wait until he gets to know the glory of *moi*! I'll break this wild stallion. In a few months, he'll be chomping at the bit, because he's never met anyone like me before." Or, "Once he matures a little, he'll realize what a catch I am. I'll just bide my time until then." Or, "The sex is so great; how could he not fall in love with me?" Every woman thinks sex is the glue, and they are so wrong. With a man, once the sex is over, it's over. He has no memory of the incident. You could be biding your time, waiting for him to realize that you're the one, until your eggs are dried up and dusty. Don't even think of making him a friend or a back-up boy. That's wasting good space in your life. So, girlfriend, spare yourself the pain and qualify the buyer before you get involved with him.

A Cautionary Tale

We've all heard horror stories about women who failed to qualify the buyer and wasted years of their lives on guys who never realized their value. A close friend of mine met and fell in love with a man from one of America's most prestigious, old-money families. You would recognize his name immediately. She was a sharp, beautiful, energetic Jew; he was a handsome, intelligent, Ivy League Protestant. They got along splendidly, reveling in the uniqueness of their differences and all they had to learn from each other, and their souls seem to meld perfectly. Although he claimed to be ready for marriage, they dated for over a year, and they never spent holidays together. She invited him to meet her family, but he didn't invite her to meet his, which is a huge red flag. When she asked him about it, he brushed her off, saying, "Let's wait until we're ready. I'll know when it's the right time." It started to eat at her. She began mentioning it fairly often, and finally she put her foot down. "Either I meet your family, or we don't move forward," she told him.

He gave in. "All right," he told her. "You want me to take you home? I'll take you home. We'll go next Saturday." They never made it through the front door. It seems his mother was extremely anti-Semitic and actually yelled at the couple, calling out racist names through the window while they stood there on the front lawn. And to make matters worse, once Mr. Fortune 500 dropped my friend off at her home that day, she never heard from him again! He never called her back to discuss closure, nothing, nada, zip. Clearly she had missed the huge blinking sign that he was not truly marriage minded. No man is who would put off introducing his girlfriend to his parents for more than a year. Obviously he knew from the get-go that it wasn't going to work. It took her a full year to get over him, but she recently ran into a Cut to the Chase Guy, who is making her feel like a million bucks.

But don't worry. I have a happy story for every horror story. Rory has been very close to me since childhood. I've been observing her dating habits for years. She had a tendency to go for the hot guy, no matter what his character was like. If he had a square jaw with a Michael Douglas dimple and thick, glossy dark hair, she was hooked. A girl can afford to play around like that until she hits her mid- to late twenties, at which time I advised her to qualify the buyer before she even accepted a date with a guy. "Find out if he's interested in marriage," I told her. "Don't even look at him if he doesn't have those qualities, no matter how physically irresistible he may seem."

She had been the classic female modelizer; I can't tell you how many male models she went out with! But she was smart enough to switch gears quickly and start paying attention to the men who might not have been so devastatingly handsome but were devastatingly marriage material. She substituted "risky" and "makes me wet at first sight" for "intelligent" and "funny." With that mind-set, she was ready for her prince when he came along. He was cute in a nerdy sort of way, positive, ambitious, athletic, and had a great sense of humor. Instead of immediately jumping into bed with him, as she had with the hot guys, she got to know this one as a friend first and qualified him over time.

The guy turned out to be rock solid—from a successful East Coast family and, get this: he was the ultimate gentleman! They finally decided to take their relationship from platonic to passionate and thought a weekend trip to a wedding upstate would be the perfect time to consummate it, if you know what I mean. He sat her down for a talk beforehand. "Rory, I'm really looking forward to this weekend," he told her. "But I just want you to know that I'm really not comfortable sleeping with you . . . unless you're my girl. We have to be involved in a monogamous, committed relationship, or it's no go." Her heart melted. She knew right then and there that he was a faithful, one-woman man. Today they're happily married and living in a beautiful home in an upscale New York suburb with three kids.

But how do you know if that adorable guy grinning at you across the table is going to be right for you? And how do you find this out before you waste two years of your life and the better portion of your heart on him? I'm going to give you a list of red flags and green lights that will either urge you to stomp on the brakes and dump this one immediately, or put the pedal to the metal and charm the pants off him before someone else does.

Red Lights

You might think these are fairly obvious, but you wouldn't believe what some women are willing to put up with. And if you believe you're above it, not so fast there, honey. Think back to the last guy you went out with. I'll bet he displayed at least one of these negative traits on the very first date, but because he was cute or sweet or dangerous or successful, you decided to give him a pass, didn't you? Now, you don't want to be too hasty about dumping a man at the slightest offense, but if any of the following traits start rearing their ugly heads too often, you should consider moving on.

PETER THE PLOTTER: Not only is he a plotter, but he's a plodder. He's all about comparison shopping, and he takes for freaking ever to make up his mind. He's usually an indecisive serial dater who tries to find value in every option and weighs it against all the others. He's the guy who will date you for a few weeks, mysteriously disappear, then several months later reappear and want to go back to the way things were before. He says he'd like to spend time with you again because he's been dating around and he hasn't found anyone else who compares to you. At this point, hopefully you'll be otherwise engaged and won't give him the time of day. He had his chance, he didn't appreciate it, and you've moved on.

FRANK THE FAUX PLANNER: He'll tell you, "Of course I want to get married, just as soon as I . . ." Finish my graduate degree, get that job, earn this promotion, etc. He's always putting important things off "just until . . ." and "until" never happens. The rotten thing about his whole routine is that he's had this all planned out from the very beginning. If you meet a man who seems to always be waiting for the ideal moment and has a million excuses for why it hasn't come along, run like you've never run before. He'll suck the life right out of a girl and leave her twisting in the wind. I don't care if he looks like Hugh Jackman, has the presence of Hugh Laurie, and the charm of Hugh Grant, kick him to the curb as quickly as possible.

FREDDY THE FRUGAL GUY: In a word, he's a cheapskate. If he's constantly complaining about money, how expensive things are, and the high cost of living, he doesn't have a generous spirit, and he'll be so busy worrying about money that he'll never notice all the wonderful things around that are free. You say, "Look at the beautiful sunset." And he says, "Yeah, those colors come from the smog in the atmosphere, caused by people driving despite the fact that gas prices are outrageous." A better man will pick up the tab when you go out to dinner with a group of friends, but not Frugal Freddy. He sits there with a calculator figuring out what everyone owes, to the penny, and even adds in a 10 percent tip (not 20 percent, mind you). Watch closely, and you'll see that the resentment he feels about the money he spends on you will start to run into other areas of your relationship.

PAULIE THE POUNCER: This guy will start saying "sex" every third word in every sentence at your first meeting, and he'll ask you all sorts of intensely intimate questions just as quickly as he can shove them into the conversation. This can be a turn-on, but know he's just interested in a quick lay and not a long-term commitment. He's the first one to tell you you're beautiful, and he'll grab you at the same time— probably your left boob. And he gets angry when you don't return the sentiment. Your first kiss will be full French, with a sloppy, wet tongue. This guy will be pushy and try to sleep with you on the first date. If you don't cooperate, he'll quickly find someone else who will. You are expendable to him. Make sure *you* expend *him* quickly.

BOBBY THE BRAGGER: He wants you to know he's a hot tamale, so he talks about other women and how they constantly pursue him. He frequently glances at the door to see if other gorgeous women have walked in, and he flirts with the waitress, bartender, hostess—anything with a vagina. He answers his cell phone and reads his text messages in the middle of a meal. He's an auditioner, the one who always says, "Let's have drinks." He might only be trying to prove to you that other women find him attractive, but he also might be in constant search of the bigger, better deal. Since there's no way of knowing his true motives, I say leave him alone.

MARK THE MISOGYNIST: He has a horrible relationship with his mother, ex-wife, and/or girlfriend, usually describes them as crazy, psycho, or bipolar, and he uses the word "bitch" a lot. He treats the female service workers around him with disdain. He has no female friends, and he resents all the women who work with him or—even worse—above him. You may think, "Well, if he really were a misogynist, what's he doing out with me?" Simply put, he's there because, while he hates your gender, he'd rather have sex with you than a gay, cross-dressing prostitute. And you're probably cheaper. Isn't that flattering? This guy sport-fucks for a living. He doesn't make love to you, he fucks you, emotionally and physically.

PIERRE THE PARTYER: This classic poser stays out late and never gets up before noon on the weekends. He wears Jack Nicholson sunglasses all the time, even indoors, and too much Ed Hardy. You're amazed at how much alcohol he can put away. You're impressed by the fact that he always picks up the tab for everyone and that he seems to know and like every single person you meet. His friends are always hard on their luck, and he tries to help them out often. He is an avid social climber and is on every party event list in town. When you go out with him, after you've had a five-course meal and your dessert drink and you're exhausted, he's ready to go out and party. "It's only two AM," he'll wheedle. "The night is young." The reason he can stay out so late is because he doesn't have a job. This guy doesn't take life seriously. He's in no way ready to settle down. He may be a good-time guy and make you laugh your ass off, but he's not a keeper.

KENNY THE CRITIC: He's full of backhanded compliments like "You look great! But I wonder how you would look with your hair up?" Or, "That dress is beautiful—do you think they have it in red?" He'll make subtle jibes at your weight ("You're not going to order dessert, are you?") and the way you speak ("Darling, your participles are dangling again."). He wants you to cut to the chase and says, "What's your point?" to get you to fast forward—he'll never let you tell a full story as he gets bored quickly. He'll try and convince you he's doing it for you own good—that he's helping you be the best person you can possibly be. But you will wind up feeling picked to death, exhausted, and resentful of him. This man is either obsessed with perfection, or he's extremely insecure, trying to place everyone at a level beneath him so he can feel superior. But this guy will end up ruining your self-esteem.

THEODORE THE THERAPIZER: He reveals fairly early on (like when he feels he needs to explain why he's not ordering a drink) that he's on antidepressants. He'll confess that he's been cheating on the shrink he sees three times a week, with another shrink. He suggests couples' therapy for the two of you by the third date (don't laugh, I have clients like this). His shelves are full of self-help books, and he's always reading the latest bestseller, but he still can't figure out why he's so messed up. You can't fix this guy, so don't even try. He doesn't need someone to help him through this hard time, no matter what he says. Gag your inner Mother Teresa and leave him to his therapist(s).

WALLY THE WOUNDED: Within the first hour of meeting him, this guy will tell you how he was abused as a kid, why his last two marriages went south, and how the doctor botched his vasectomy. You may misinterpret this, thinking that you feel so comfortable with each other so fast that you can reveal everything—that's where you get in trouble. You'll find yourself revealing way more about yourself than you should to him, and you'll scare each other off. This guy is not unpacking his baggage all over the table because he trusts and values honesty—it's not a compliment. He's telling you about his life's woes because he's not over them yet! Tell him to try back in six months when his wounds aren't so fresh.

PHIL THE FLAKE: He cancels at the last minute repeatedly because of a work thing, a family emergency, or a relative's death (I dated a guy who once used the death in the family excuse three times in one week.) If he doesn't show up when he says he will and doesn't call, it's even worse, and you shouldn't give him a second chance. This guy is probably still in love with his ex and she's pulling his chain. Or maybe he's one of those people who just doesn't honor his word, or forgets it as soon as he gives it. He's the classic Best Offer Boy, which means he's constantly looking for a better offer and will double or triple book a night. I have many clients like this. Who has time for this passive-aggressive behavior? Delete him from your life immediately.

COLBY THE CONTROL FREAK: The good thing about this guy is that he's prompt. The bad thing about him is that he will never forgive you if you're not—even if you're only a few minutes late. You can tell a control freak right off the bat by the way he insists on sitting in what he considers just the right chair at a very specific table in a restaurant, and he'll ask to be moved several times if he's not satisfied. He'll also make a production of straightening the silverware. You may think he truly cares about you when he gives you that cell phone as a gift, but he really wants to be able to check up on you any time, anywhere, to make sure you're doing something he approves of. He'll try to control what you eat, what you wear, how you spend your time, etc. The only woman he's good for is one that doesn't have a mind of her own and enjoys being bossed around. The fact that you're reading this book tells me that obviously that isn't you.

Green Lights

Be on the lookout for these sure signs that he's a marriage-minded man and not simply a playa. Remember, **you don't want a player, you want a stayer.** Even if he's not particularly floating your boat, qualify him as a good option for one of your friends. You can either pay it forward or get a referral from him for his handsome friends.

QUINTON THE QUALIFIER: He knows exactly what he wants, and he wants it yesterday. If you don't fit his ideal, he won't waste your time, he'll quickly move on. He'll ask you all the qualifying questions in the first few weeks, or days, of knowing him. "Do you want children?" "How do you feel about settling down?" "Do you want to work or stay at home and raise kids?" "If my job took me to Alaska, would you be willing to move?" Those are all the questions you were going to ask him, and it's fair to turn them around and ask him the same things. It might feel like "21 Questions" and you could get exhausted from the process, but fear not, this is a seriously marriage-minded man, and if you make the cut, he could be your husband by Valentine's Day. He's ready to settle down and he doesn't want to waste any time. This man is on a marriage mission. You might be tempted to tell him what you think he wants to hear because he seems like such a sincere guy and you don't want to lose him by giving him any "wrong" answers. But it's very important that you be 100 percent honest with him. He's qualifying you, just as you're qualifying him. Better not to waste each other's time if your life goals don't mesh.

CARL THE CONSISTENT: If you find a guy who calls when he says he will and takes you out on a regular basis, I don't care if he's a three-eyed dwarf, nab him! He's going to make a great husband. He's probably successful in his job because he is a hard worker and always does what he says he'll do. He'll make you feel great during courtship, because no week will go by without a special date, no day will go by without a phone call, even if he's not a talker, he'll just want to check in. He'll plan trips and weekend getaways for you well in advance. If he's a twenty-something, he's the consummate texter. He likes to know where you are at all times. Give him a chance, even if he doesn't make your toes curl in the beginning. A guy like this will grow on you.

FINN THE FINE DINER: The man who sees that you're well fed is a generous man who will nurture you and be proud of it. Even if he cooks for you at home and doesn't take you out to the fanciest restaurants, he's still showing that he's interested in your physical well-being and ready to take responsibility for it. By the way, never trust a man who doesn't enjoy his food, someone who picks at it or wolfs it down is surely not into sensual pleasure. Finn the Fine Diner orders two desserts and wants to share them so he can spoon-feed you the whipped cream. He eats with zest and relishes his food, which is a sign he'll be great in the sack. He's the guy who will pick up the tab for you and your girlfriends, even though you met up with him later and you didn't have dinner with him.

SPENCER THE SELF-MADE MAN: He's the guy for whom I coined the phrase providership. He may not have an education, but he will always take care of his woman. She will never do without. If he has an education, you're on a rich rocket to the stars, because this guy has ambition. He may or may not have a great relationship with his parents, so if you're the opposite of what his mother dreamed of for him, he'll still pick you. He's marching to the beat of a different drummer. He is a leader. The man who has managed to pull himself up by his own bootstraps knows that if he works at something hard enough, he can succeed. He'll bring this attitude into marriage. He won't cave at the first little challenge; he'll figure out a way to get past it. He's aggressive and sometimes a little bit sales-y but he's the guy with the charm, and you'll always have a lot of laughter in your life. Mr. Self-Made comes in all different shapes, sizes, ethnic and religious backgrounds, but the common denominator is that he has done it on his own, depends on no one, and is always resourceful. Truer lyrics were never written than, "Mama may have, and Papa may have, but God bless the child that's got his own."

OSCAR THE OPTIMIST: It's a great pleasure to be around someone who tries to find the good in everything around him—especially when that applies to you. He believes in you and encourages you. He believes in himself and has contagious confidence in his ability to make things work. He believes in the joy of matrimony, and knows that it's out there waiting for him. Best of all, he'll tell you you're beautiful, even when you're bloated and your hair's dirty and you're wearing your shot-elastic granny panties. Oscar is a pleaser and will definitely work to give you the big O. He's also the one who says, "Hey, you wanna go back to school? Don't worry about it, I'll support you." He'll run to the store and pick up the Tampax and Midol when you're having a PMS meltdown, and when you have kids he'll always make them smile. Oh, and don't forget, he helps out around the house!

DANNY THE DIVORCÉ: He's the first and quickest to get married, because he hates being alone, unless he comes from a bitter, negative divorce, in which case you'd know better than to be on a date with him anyway. Don't consider the ex-wife and kids a burden, consider them a blessing in that they've introduced him to the joys of family life, and he'll usually be eager to get back into it. He feels lonely and incomplete without a family, or at least a wife, by his side. He's family oriented and definitely a homeowner. Even if he loses his big, beautiful house in his divorce, he'll get another one, probably close to his ex so he can easily visit the kids. Speaking of kids, he wants to have more. He likes you to come along with him when he does domestic errands like grocery shopping, dropping off the dry cleaning, and filling the tank at the gas station. And if you're lucky and his ex is already in a relationship or married, he's quickest to close the deal. Haven't you ever noticed how quickly divorced men get married again? They'll meet and marry a woman in a tenth of the time it will take an eternal bachelor to settle down with the right girl. This guy has a history of committing, and the concept of partnering with someone is not foreign to him. If he doesn't yammer about his ex-wife all the time, this one can be a real find.

GARY THE GREAT FRIEND: He's the guy who has been hanging in there trying to get you to notice him, or the guy who's always been in another relationship before and is now free to spend time with you. Or maybe he was a coworker who transferred away or changed positions and is now free to date you without repercussions. He's slow and steady, a movie-and-popcorn guy, but he's the one you can count on when you're stuck on the highway with a flat tire at 2:00 AM and he's the one that remembers your birthday when the guy you're dating doesn't and brings you a Cheesecake Factory Oreo Mudslide Cheesecake. He's the one who will take you to a concert when your favorite musician is in town. Give him bonus points if he has good, upstanding friends of both sexes, both married and single. Give him even more points if some of his friends are much older than he his, or much younger. This means that he is flexible and can get along with just about anyone. If he is committed to his friends and introduces you to them, you've hit the jackpot.

LINK THE LANDOWNER: Even if it's a small studio condo, he who has invested in real estate knows the joys of investing in the future. He refuses to pay rent, thinking that is simply wasting his hard-earned cash. He's the teenager who took the paper route to save money to buy his first car. He often dreams about getting out of the big city and buying a big parcel of land where he'll build his dream house. When he signs up for the thirty-year mortgage, he signs up for his wife. He has made a commitment and is probably living with(in) it. Purchasing property is the male version of nesting, even if it's not the cleanest, most organized, or well-decorated place you've ever seen. One of my friends is a fifty-five-year-old bachelor, never been married, but he is so ready to tie the knot his teeth hurt. He has a grand house in the Hollywood Hills, the walls are decorated with Warhols, Lichtensteins, and Picassos, and while his kitchen is nothing to brag about, he's ready, willing, and waiting for his wife to design a new one to her own specifications.

VINNIE THE VOLUNTEER: If he enthusiastically tells you he works for a cause in his spare time, know that you've got a man with a heart of gold. He could just as easily be shooting hoops with his buddies and drinking beer, but this guy. is spending his Saturday mornings helping with dog adoptions, hiking with a Little Brother, or canvassing a neighborhood for some bill he's passionate about getting passed. Often the corporate raider, his real dream is to start a nonprofit, check out of the fast lane, make his own schedule, and get on the road with his wife, helping humanity. He's a do-gooder, he's giving back to the community, and he's thinking about something other than himself or getting laid. I say, offer to volunteer along with him. It is a great way to get to know someone. Some great charities to get involved with include Habitat for Humanity, where you'll find the rugged, muscle-bound Mr. Fix-it types. The Lance Armstrong Foundation attracts Hollywood stars and the athletic do-gooder, and you'll find the man who loves children volunteering for Make-A-Wish.

JONATHAN THE GENTLEMAN: Let him be your knight in shining armor. The man who feels chivalrous is the man who feels love. Please don't penalize him because he's decided to put you on a pedestal and treat you like a jewel to be adorned. For all you strict, equality-minded feminists who aren't married, how's that working for you? Know that you *can* have your cake and eat it too, with equal pay for equal work, and still have your car door opened while being treated like a princess. So many men are confused these days, and it's our own fault. There are actually women out there who say, "I can open the door for myself, thank you," and "Excuse me? I'm perfectly capable of ordering my own food." The poor guy is only trying to be the gentleman his mother taught him to be, and we are ruining him and confusing him by not allowing him these little acts of chivalry. Then we punish him in our PMS moments when he doesn't drop everything for us. Blessed is the man who has been rebuffed by bitter women's libbers but still insists on being a gentleman by helping you with your coat or getting the door for you. He is a nurturer and a caretaker and should be encouraged.

Ten Must-Haves, Five Non-Negotiables

Even though you're sitting at a candlelit table with a Landowning Volunteer Gentleman Optimist, you still might find there's something missing. For some strange reason you just can't understand why. Fear not, my friend. We're all subject to our own, unique deal breakers—those specific qualities or traits that a man must have for us to even consider him. For some, it's the desire to raise children. For others, it's similar religious beliefs. Believe it or not, smoking is a common deal breaker with men. I know one woman who firmly believes a bald patch is a deal breaker. (She's still single, by the way). You need to decide what your deal breakers are, and you must never even lick the earlobe of anyone who doesn't add up. To better define your own deal breakers, try the following exercise:

Pull out the winners and losers lists that you created during Dating Detox. Review the positives you wrote down and decide whether you want to omit or add any. Now flip all the negatives you wrote down on the losers list into positives. For example, if you've always dated cool, aloof, and indifferent men, then what you are really looking for is a sexy, warm, nurturing man. Now merge those lists and make a five-column table like the one I've shown here, with the Five Worlds from Step One heading each column: Spiritual, Physical, Emotional, Intellectual, and Financial. Decide which five traits are most important in each and list them in order of priority:

SPIRITUAL	PHYSICAL	EMOTIONAL	INTELLECTUAL	FINANCIAL
1.	1.	1.	1.	1.
2.	2.	2.	2.	2.
3.	3.	3.	3.	3.
4.	4.	4.	4.	4.
5.	5.	5.	5.	5.

Take note of whether you have trouble filling up one of the categories. For instance, if it takes you forever to come up with five intellectual traits that matter to you, then your emphasis is not on the intellectual. If you fill in the physical in five seconds, that's probably where your priority is.

FYI, do not be embarrassed to write down some of the things that women are afraid to ask for because they feel they're being greedy or inconsiderate, such as money. If his finances aren't where you want them to be and he has no desire to make more, your marriage will not be able to sustain the test of time. I should know, I'm the Millionaire Matchmaker. Also, don't be afraid to put down that he needs to want to get married soon. That's not being desperate. If you want to get married now, and he wants to get married seven years from now, he is not your guy, and you should not buy into him saying "If you really love me, you'll wait." You must listen to your inner clock and love yourself first, otherwise you will come to resent him. Another trait that you shouldn't be embarrassed about wanting is being cosmopolitan. If you're a city girl glamazon who loves her Jimmy Choos and her Balenciaga bags, loves to go to the theater, can't live without her Frappuccinos from Starbucks, and hates the thought of moving to the suburbs or the country, then clearly Mr. Farmer Country Boy is not for you.

The one thing you can't put in any column is chemistry. You've got to leave that to God, because it's indefinable. It's the magic you must leave to the universe to supply. It's why you find yourself attracted to someone you would not normally be drawn to. "I don't know what it is about him, but he just does it for me." It's the fairy dust—let the fairies have some wriggle room.

You now have a list of twenty-five qualities that are important to you. Take a look at the chart you've made, and pick the ten traits that are most crucial.

Ten Must-Haves
1.
2.
3.
4.
5.
6.
7.
8.
9.
10.

These qualities are your **Ten Must-Haves** that the mate of your dreams must have in order to be a perfect fit. But you can change this list from time to time as you evolve, grow, and mature, and perhaps you'll be able to negotiate on them a bit. For example, if he's a little short in the financial world but he has tons of ambition, you can live with that, especially if he's in his twenties and just entering the work force.

My own personal list changed as I became more financially successful. Back when I was just starting out in my career, it didn't matter to me if he made more money than I did—we could both be young, ambitious, and brimming with potential. But at this time in my life, he damn well better have delivered on some of that potential and be making at least as much, if not more, than I do. I find that men become dependent and intimidated, give off feminine energy, and start feeling a very unattractive sense of entitlement when I'm the one making the most money in the relationship. I simply cannot deal with that.

The top five entries on that list are your **Five Non-Negotiables**, and you cannot compromise on these. They are the absolute most important traits in a mate, and if the guy you're seeing doesn't have them, you need to move on. Yesterday. No exceptions. If wanting children is number two on your list and he doesn't want them at all, unless you're willing to compromise by getting a dog, then he's not your guy.

As a matter of fact, don't even get started with anyone who doesn't have all five of your Non-Negotiables. Don't give out your phone number, don't meet for coffee, don't encourage him in any way whatsoever.

This is so important that I want you to write your Five Non-Negotiables on a card, laminate it, and carry it around with you in your purse, backpack, or pocket at all times. Take it out and look at it constantly. If you meet someone and he doesn't have the five, but you're tempted because he's cute, reread your card, chant it like a mantra, do whatever it takes to kick his ass to the curb. Remember you're on a marriage mission and you don't have time to waste.

This may sound harsh, but believe me, I'm saving you a lot of heartache. Think of how much easier it will be to nip him in the bud, so to speak, than to break up with him ten months later because it's obvious you don't want the same things. We've all violated this rule and wish we hadn't. So often we make exceptions because, again, we think we can change him. We tell ourselves, "He says he doesn't want children, but when he sees what a great mother I can be and how a child could complete his life, he'll come around." Sure—go ahead and get pregnant. You'll be singing a different tune after he's left you for a hot, childless model and you have to put his name on the Deadbeat Dad's list because you're still waiting for the child support payments. You should not try to change him. And if you stick hard and fast to your Five Non-Negotiables, you will never have to go through the frustration of trying to change him. I'll repeat this several more times before this book is through, because it's one of the most important messages you'll read. The best benefit of making this list is that you will no longer notice the losers and start attracting the winners.

Note to Women over Forty:

While we're on the topic of how our needs and expectations change as we grow in wisdom and experience (notice I didn't say, "as we get older" or "as we age"), I want to tell those of you who are forty and over, *please, do not panic*! By this time in your life, whether you've been married to a loser, or three, or have never been married, there is still plenty of hope. Do not give up or desperately glom onto the first marriage-minded man who comes along. You still have every right to qualify the buyer, and I have a special strategy for you: shop older.

I'm talking ten to fifteen years older. There are infinite advantages to this. Most men who are fifty plus are more secure—both financially and socially. They've already proven themselves so they're not spending twenty hours a day at the office, and they're ready to settle down and enjoy the fruits of their labors. They're looking for a friend, a travel companion—someone who can appreciate the restaurants and other lovely things they can finally afford. Men over fifty know how to court a woman, and they're all too well aware of what *doesn't* work. They're usually past their "I wanna date a *Playboy* model" stage, because they've dated younger women and realize that they have nothing in common and have a hard time keeping up. Many of my older members of the Millionaire's Club will only date women over forty—they tell me not to even think of introducing them to anyone younger because they want a wife, not a daughter. I'm more than happy to accommodate their wishes.

And don't believe for a second that older men are past their sexual prime. These guys have taken the time and effort to know their way around a woman's body. As long as the little blue pill is on the market, these men can rise to the occasion. They realize they don't have the stamina they did when they were younger, so they make up for it with sensitivity, finesse, and romance. They're not so focused on coming—they're more about the journey. Do not penisize, I mean penalize, him for taking Viagra or anything like it. He's doing it to please you, my dear. I'm just sorry they haven't perfected a similar medication for women. Everyone needs a little boost every now and then. There are always women over forty who argue with me over this, saying, "I'm over forty and I'm in great shape. I want a guy who is the same age or younger!" I say that if you want to date a man who is your age or younger, fine, go ahead. But be forewarned: you're likely to run into a couple of problems. First off, marriage-minded men under forty who want to get married and raise a family are not going to be all that interested in you. I hate to say it, but your prime childbearing years are numbered, and the girls under forty have the advantage. In vitro, adoption, and fertility treatments are expensive, stressful, and time consuming. Many men don't want to take the chance of going there if they don't have to. You can't argue with biology.

Are there exceptions to this? Of course, but by the time you find that one-in-a-million guy who's willing to overlook your age, you could be well into your sixties. So that leaves you with younger men who are not marriage minded, and chances are you're more successful and secure than they are. You could easily find yourself playing the part of sugar mamma, with a hot young stud drinking cappuccino on your couch while you run off to work. If you're one of those women in her forties who always dates younger men and can never close the deal, why not try a man ten to fifteen years older? He might surprise you with a ring.

Women truly are like a fine wine that improves with age. Beyond the joys of dating men over fifty, let's take a look at the advantages that women forty-plus have over their little sisters:

1. They've come into their own. The anxiety of youth is gone, and women over forty often have the experience and maturity to be calm and relax.

2. They know their bodies. They have an idea of what pleases them and how to please a man. They're usually past the childish, self-conscious stage, and have a better knowledge of how to use their sexual power. No longer do the C-section scar, the droopy breasts, and the extra love in the handles bother them.

3. They're better at conversation. As men age and testosterone levels decrease, they're more focused on someone they can talk to. They're no longer in a relationship focused on bedroom acrobatics; they want someone who's fun to chat with—and who is also comfortable with silence.

4. They're less impetuous. Women over forty are less inclined to volatile mood swings, explosive anger, and

puzzling irrationality. They're past the flaky stage that my male clients complain about.

Now that you know yourself oh-so-much better, and you're aware of how to qualify the buyer, it's time to go out and touch, smell, and play with the merchandise. Strap yourself in, you are about to embark on Adventures in Dating.

STEP FIVE

Adventures in Dating

I have a confession to make. Right here, right now, I'm going to let you in on my dirty little secret. Ready? Here it goes: I hate dating. I really, really do. I would rather sit through ten hours of simultaneous electrolysis, liposuction, and bikini waxing than go on a first, second, or third date. Believe me, no one hates dating more than I do.

The upside is that if I can learn how to enjoy dating, anyone can. And I did. Think of it this way: the more you hate dating, the more inclined you will be to do what it takes to get it over with and settle down in a healthy, happy, monogamous relationship. You'll never end up in the same boat as Lisa, who was one of those rare birds who absolutely loved dating. She loved dating so much she would go out three times a day, seven days a week if she didn't have to show up at the office every day. Those first dates with a new guy was what really turned her on. The first meeting, the first eye lock, the first touch, the first kiss. She became addicted to the adrenalin rush of all the firsts, and by the thirds she was bored stiff and ready to seek the new thrill again. Although she loved dressing up and going out to dinner, she wasn't attracting serious men, only the looky-loos—the ninety-day wonder guys who disappeared at the three-month mark.

It wasn't until she was in her late forties that she finally decided to settle down and take my advice. Although she was my friend, I never realized how much she loved Jewish men; the problem was she was a lapsed Protestant. My mom would boast to her at family functions that Jewish men make the best husbands. So one day, on a dare, I told her to get her blond shiksa self onto JDate. Now you must understand, the website was originally designed to keep Jewish singles from interfaith marriage, but women of all faiths started to sign up. The men welcomed them with open arms and Lisa was no exception. She found plenty of nonpracticing Jews who didn't mind the shiksa invasion. Jim, a handsome, fifty-something producer, was sick of the Flaky Friedas in Los Angeles, and needed someone who challenged his mind but couldn't care less about religion. The minute he laid eyes on Lisa's profile with her long, flowing blond hair, her plastic-surgery-free, fit body, and her razor-sharp mind, he was smitten. Both were having the worst dating year of their lives and were beginning to think that there's no such thing as a soul mate. On their first dinner date they thought, "Wow! What was that?" Five dates later they both knew that this would be it. While the baby boat had left the dock, Lisa was extremely fortunate to find a great husband when she was good and ready, and they're now very happily married. At their ages, they knew exactly what they wanted, and they didn't waste any time once they found it. This is a prime example of what I call Shaking the Tree. This means going outside your comfort zone when your usual methods of dating are not working for you.

Lisa was doing one thing right, though (before I got a hold of her): she was going out on *lots* of dates. Dating is a numbers game and the more men you go out with, the more likely you are to find your mate. I know, I know, women today are exhausted from work, paying the bills, and social obligations. Life is more complicated than ever, and just surviving can suck the energy right out of you. On top of that, you're probably tired of doing the same thing over and over again— meeting a guy, spending money that you don't have on clothes and beauty treatments, getting ready, spending the whole evening explaining who you are, and trying to make a good impression. Just writing about it makes me want to go get a massage and facial. So if you're really going to do this thing called dating, you better make it fun. You better find a way to get at least something satisfying out of every date you endure, so in the end you can feel grateful to the universe for providing you with a new opportunity, rather than pissed that you just wasted six hours of your life that you'll never get back with a complete jerk.

Dating Data

One of the best tricks I play on myself to help me actually enjoy the dating process is to gather and record as much Dating Data as possible. What is Dating Data? It is all the new information you obtain as a result of going out on these dates. Remember, you can learn something from everyone, and knowledge and experience are invaluable—your date is going to give you something precious no matter what he's like. You can also see to it that you get something positive out of the place or activity the two of you have selected. If he takes you to a restaurant you've never been to before and you order something delicious that you've never had the chance, or courage to try, well, then at least *something* good came from it. This worked for me beyond belief when I moved to Los Angeles from Miami, and I encourage all the girls in the Millionaire's Club to do it, so they'll be happy and engaging during their dates, rather than bored and resentful. Remember, even if you think the guy you're out with is a total waste of oxygen, you never know who he knows—his brother could be your Prince Charming.

Right now I want you to grab a pen and paper, or sit down in front of your computer, and make a dating wish list. Write down a list of fun activities you've always wanted to try, like film festivals, concerts, wine tastings, sporting events, plays, boating, skiing, sushi making, cigar smoking, the sky's the limit—but wait, it doesn't have to be—what about sky diving or helicopter touring? Use a city guide to help you with this. Nothing's too good for you or beyond your reach—these are all activities that take a lot of planning, and things you normally wouldn't do for yourself. That's why it's called a wish list.

Now write down the names of all the restaurants you've wanted to try, ranging from the hole in the wall to the most posh five-star in town. How about that Mexican dive where they have chile relleno burritos the size of a football player's forearm? Or that new raw foods place you've heard so much about? That cute little mountain tavern? The barbecue place out on the highway? The biker bar where they serve the best burgers on this side of the Mississippi? That world renowned, haute cuisine establishment you saw featured on the Food Network? Make a list a mile long.

Once you have these lists of activities and restaurants, you'll be fully prepared when a man asks you, as he inevitably will, "What would you like to do? Where would you like to go? What kind of food do you like to eat?" When a man asks you out, he wants to please you, and he's sincere in his openness to suggestions. You're making it easier on him by coming up with your own ideas and ensuring that at the very least you'll walk away from the date with new Dating Data. The conversation should go something like this:

HIM: What would you like to do?

YOU: You sound like a pretty resourceful guy, I'm open. (Compliment him, and let him make the first suggestion.)

HIM: (He'll probably take a moment to process. Don't interrupt him. This silence means he likes you and is working on it.) Then he'll say, "Any suggestions for where you want to go?"

YOU: (Then you hit him with what you want.) "Well, I'm a big fan of sushi. Have you been to the new Katsu-Ya yet?"

HIM: No—I'll make reservations right now.

The marriage-minded, hunter man jumps on the suggestion. Otherwise he'll say something like, "No, that's too expensive," or, "I don't want to drive that far."

Also, you should be prepared with an alternative just in case he suggests that awful Thai place where your cousin got food poisoning. You can say something like, "Oh, yes—I've heard about that restaurant. You know, what I'd really like to try is . . ." and suggest another restaurant in the same price range.

Here's an example of how this works to help you better appreciate the dating experience: I was lined up with a friend of a friend, who I'd heard was the ultimate wine snob. It didn't exactly sound like a match, but I'd always wanted to learn more about wine, so when he asked me where I'd like to meet, I suggested a restaurant I'd heard had a killer wine list, and he was impressed! When we met, we both knew immediately that it wasn't going to be a love match—no chemistry whatsoever on either one of our parts. But we still had an enjoyable evening together. I picked his brain about wine, and he was happy to share his knowledge. It made him feel smart, sophisticated, and important. Besides, he was happy to have an appreciative dinner companion with whom he could share a great bottle of wine, regardless of the fact that he wasn't going to get a little sumpthin' sumpthin' at the end of the evening. This guy was the best buddy of one of my closest friend's husbands—had I been rude to him, they would have been insulted and never introduced me to anyone ever again. Although the sparks didn't fly between us, I obtained exceptional Dating Data and would now know what kind of wine to order the next time I was out on a date, and he didn't have to eat dinner alone. It was a win/win situation, for which I am grateful to this very day.

You can find something good in every situation if you're inclined to do so. One of the girls in my club had an insanely mismatched blind date at Topanga Canyon's beautiful Inn of the Seventh Ray (not with one of my clients—I would never do that to anyone I know). While she really had to use all her skill, concentration, and effort to be engaged and engaging, she remembered the incredible food and the supremely romantic ambience, and ended up getting married there several years later. This is a classic example of the benefits of gathering Dating Data. You go to a place that you love with the wrong guy, then you use the invaluable information you gather there with the right guy, and you create a better memory.

The bottom line is that if you walk away with a positive, grateful, cheerful attitude, word will spread. When someone does the dating equivalent of a Google search on you, you'll always come up flawless. Singles news travels fast no matter where you live. Small town or big city, if you're known for being someone who is always gracious on a date, your dating reputation will shine, and your opportunities will grow. Men talk—don't let anyone tell you they don't.

The 4:1 Rule

After all this talk about him taking you places, it's time for you to reciprocate and do something nice for him. I call it the

4:1 Rule: every four times he takes you out, whether it's to dinner, the movies, ice cream, whatever, you must give something back to him, but you can't top him. The woman who gives more than the man in a relationship reverses the masculine/feminine roles. First the man will appreciate it, then he'll expect it, and eventually he'll resent it.

Also, she who touches money gives off masculine energy, so you can't physically touch cash before his eyes or whip out the plastic to pay the check. Why? Because, as I've noted, the man is the hunter, the woman is the gatherer, and the man is supposed to provide for the woman. So if she begins providing for him, it throws everything off balance. (Once you're in a committed relationship, however, a partnership develops and things change—you'll have discussed who takes care of what financially.) So, how do you give back if you can't spend money? You make him dinner. You bake him his favorite cookies. You pick up his shirts from the cleaner because he can't get there in time. You help him clean his house. You download his favorite songs on his iPod. You send him an e-greeting (they're free!).

If you feel he's spent exorbitant amounts of money on you and you want to show your appreciation, you may purchase clothing for him, his favorite aftershave, tickets to the theater or a concert (let him hold the tickets, however—that makes him feel like a man). Under no circumstance, even if you're a millionairess, should you spend more money on him than he did on you, or kidnap him and take him away on a lavish vacation. Those things are saved for monogamy, not for the first stages of courtship. If he whines about the fact that he's spending more money than you are and you're not spending enough, tell him, "You have every right to feel the way you do, but I'm a traditional girl, and I don't feel comfortable paying for dates. I will understand if you would like to date someone else who will." Awkward silence will ensue. Do not say anything. Check out emotionally and mentally—plan what you're going to wear to work tomorrow. If he's serious about you, he will understand and never bring up the subject again. However, you may be dining at Olive Garden and not Spago in the future. If he continues to whine, he's a cheap bastard who will not make you feel taken care of—not just financially, but emotionally too, and you should get rid of him.

Dating Do's and Don'ts

Now that you've got the right attitude, let's talk a little about dating etiquette. Best-case scenario: after the first date, you want a second, third, and fourth and he's begging you for more. You don't want to blow it by doing or saying something that breaks the deal before it's even on the table.

I know you're going to resist this, but know that as women, our mouths get us in a lot of trouble. We're often uncomfortable with silence, and we feel the need to say something, anything, to keep the conversation going, and we stick our feet, or our purses, or our elbows, in our mouths, without even realizing what we've done. I've made the following list of topics you should definitely avoid on the first date . . . or the second . . . or the third. For God's sake, some of these things you shouldn't even talk about after you've been married for ten years.

Never talk about:

YOUR OWN ADVENTURES IN DATING: Sometimes, in an effort to appear desirable, self-deprecating, entertaining, whatever, women will talk about their dating history, both good and bad. Think about it: if you try to regale him with stories of dating disasters, he's going to get the impression you have bad dating karma. If you tell him about all the great places other men have taken you, he's going to be intimidated. Even though you both know it's not true, every man wants to feel like he's the only man you've ever had fun with on a date. The minute you start talking about your dating history, you neutralize his sexual desire, and move into the friend zone.

YOUR EX: If I had a dollar for every time one of my club members, no matter the gender, blew a date by complaining about an ex, I'd be driving a Ferrari right now. They whine about getting over a bad breakup in an effort to induce sympathy, or they want to make it clear from the very beginning that they won't put up with certain behavior, or, most boring of all, they're still not over their last relationship and they want a shoulder to cry on. By the way, if he is prattling on and on about his ex and you're just about ready to slit your own throat with the butter knife, here's a perfect way to change the subject: "Wow, that sounds like a very difficult situation, but what I'd really like to talk about is you—you're the fascinating one." This rule also applies if he's trying to get information out of you. So, say he's probing you for information about your ex you don't want to share, and you've tried to change the subject but to no avail, here's what you say: "You know what? I'm just not the type of girl who kisses and tells. The past is the past, and what's important is that I'm here with YOU now."

MONEY: You might be trying to find out what he makes. You might be trying to impress him with your own salary or a recent deal you closed. You might just be wondering if he's okay with your ordering an appetizer *and* an entrée. Whatever you do, do not talk about money. Do not talk about how much or how little something costs, and above all, never ask. Talking about money is considered extremely crass by those who have it, and extremely threatening by those who don't. Only the most naïve and unsophisticated ask, "What did you pay for that?" or, "I bet you make a really good living doing that, right?" Talking about money is so uncouth, yet so prevalent. The absolute worst is asking a man for money at any time during the relationship. I'll go so far as to kick a girl out of the Millionaire's Club if a man reports she asked him for anything of monetary value. "I ain't sayin' she's a gold digger, but . . ." If you lead with your money foot, you'll zap the romance, send the relationship right into business mode, and bring on instant below-the-belt deflation.

HEALTH PROBLEMS: Eventually, if you have a debilitating condition, you'll have to share it with your man, but for heaven's sake, to come right out with, "I have cramps—it's that time of month, you know," or, "You don't want to get too close—I've been hacking and sniffling all week," is just plain crazy, and you can add insanity to your list of maladies. I know, this sounds like common sense to some, but think of how many times you hear someone you've only just met blurt out information like this, and you're not even on a date. I recently attended an important business meeting where one woman announced, "Sorry I'm late, but it's really hard for me to get anywhere on time today. I went on a hike this weekend and got blisters all over my feet, and they're just popping and oozing all over the place, and I shouldn't even be wearing shoes, let alone walking." Imagine how attractive that made her sound to the men, and even the women, in the meeting. It's no surprise that she's single, even though she's reasonably attractive.

Unfortunately you'll find many men who are big babies about their health, and they'll go on and on about it if you let them. It was a way to get attention and sympathy from their mommies when they were young, and now they're trying to use that same technique on you. They will go on long health tirades, but don't give in to the temptation to join them. "You think you're allergic? You should see what happens to ME when I eat shellfish!" It's never a good idea to talk about yourself in unflattering terms on any subject, at least in the beginning.

RELIGION: Even if you and your date are of the same faith, and it's a big part of both of your lives, it's not a good idea to get into deep, emotionally charged conversations too quickly. It instigates false bonding and will cause you to overlook many other glaring flaws, simply because you have this one, very important issue in common. And if it's really important to you that you share the same beliefs, you should know the basics about each other before you even go out on the first date.

POLITICS: Eventually you'll probably have a great time discussing your opinions, both similar and different, about politics. But in the beginning, this is such a heated topic your fragile relationship might not be able to suffer the heat. My ex-boyfriend and I, for example, almost came to tears and blows and we certainly didn't refrain from shouting, when we were discussing our differences of opinion about Hillary Clinton and Barack Obama. I was so passionate about the whole issue I had to keep reminding myself, "It's okay to disagree . . . this is the man I love." There is no way our relationship would have survived the primaries had we not been dating for four years prior.

NEGATIVE SUBJECTS THAT DEPRESS YOU: In the beginning, it's very important to be upbeat and engaging. You don't want to appear ponderous and overburdened by the worries of the world. We humans tend to gravitate toward those who buoy us up, rather than drag us down. No one likes a wet blanket. You want him to come away from the first date feeling happy and uplifted, not depressed, guilty, and inadequate because he cannot instantly solve all the world's problems. He wants to be your hero, your knight in shining armor—and if he gets the impression that your multiple dragons are beyond his ability to slay, he'll feel impotent, and therefore unattracted to you. One of the girls in my club had never even been to New Orleans, but for some reason Hurricane Katrina hit her hard, and she was completely devastated by it. For months it was all she talked about, on dates, at work, when she was out with her girlfriends, everywhere. People started avoiding her, because she was making them feel guilty and depressed that they weren't doing more—it was hard to have a good time around her. When one of my male clients reported back to me, "I wrote a thousand dollar check to the relief fund she was working with just to get out of there. I'd really rather not see her again," I took her aside and told her she might want to be a little more upbeat.

YOUR CHILDREN: Don't lead with them—they'll eventually come up in conversation, but if the first thing out of your mouth is "I only have a few hours—babysitter, you know . . ." you've indicated right up front that your date is an inconvenience and he's coming between you and your children. If you gush on and on about your kids, and immediately take out your wallet to show pictures, he'll get the same impression. Shauna, a member of my club who looks like Jennifer Garner and Salma Hayek combined, has a beautiful big house, and still models full time, leads conversations with "I have five kids, you probably don't want to date me, do you?" She thinks she's tricking the man if she doesn't reveal that immediately, but it prevents her from moving past the first phone call and allowing the man the chance to really get to know her. There's nothing wrong with talking about kids eventually, you just don't want to bombard anyone at the very beginning.

Also, you need to be able to mentally separate yourself from your children for a few hours at the very least, or you're not ready to start dating. Going on a date is not unlike going to work. You don't think and talk about your children the whole time you're on the job, do you? Even if your date has children too and seems more than happy to compare parenting notes, you could find that at the end of the date you know all about his children, but nothing about him. Also, talking too much about your kids too soon encourages making the huge mistake of introducing the kids to your romantic interest before any of you are ready.

SEX: If you're very comfortable with your own sexuality, sex might be one of your favorite subjects—it's arousing, titillating, and superstimulating. A guy will notice this, and egg you on. If the conversation gets overly charged, it's going to be tough not to indulge in some of those fantasies you've been talking about—especially if alcohol is flowing. Have you ever been sitting in a restaurant, and he gets this wicked little twinkle in his eye and starts talking about something really sexy, and you can't help but go there too, and before you know it you're making out right there at the table, he's groping you with one hand and with the other hand he's signaling the waiter to bring the check? I've been there, and I have to tell you it's almost impossible not to consummate your passion after that. Best to avoid the subject until you're in a better position to fulfill your fantasies. However, it's okay to flirt—be sensual, but classy.

YOUR DIET: An unfortunate truth is that losing weight seems to be one of most women's favorite topics of conversation. We scrutinize our food for protein, carbs, fat, roughage, sugar, salt, mercury, additives, and countless other factors before we put the first bite in our mouths. I bet you spend an inordinate amount of time with your girlfriends discussing food and how it affects your figure, the latest diet craze, how this star or that lost so much weight so fast, colonics, etc. Do not share this information with your date! This is one of the most boring topics in the world to men, and if you discuss it too much, he's going to think you're prone to obesity at the slightest whiff of dessert. You will train him to watch every bite that goes into your mouth with more scrutiny than you do, and the last thing you want to hear from your boyfriend is, "Are you really going to eat that?"

Also, if you have specific dietary issues, such as lactose intolerance, diabetes, allergies, or even if you're kosher, vegetarian, or vegan, you don't want to dwell on this. If something you can't eat is offered to you, politely decline, and don't go into detail unless your date specifically asks you about it. The last thing he needs from you is a lecture about the evils of alcohol, or the cruelty of eating anything with a face. Belle, a supermodel who is a member of my club, makes her strategic way of eating an issue during the first phone call. First she tells them she can't eat past 7:00 PM, then she tells them she's a vegetarian, don't even try to tempt her with the calamari, then she tells them that if he does eat meat, she will not be kissing him that night, and last but not least, she tells him about her experience at the Optimum Health Institute, where she found out that shellfish stays in your body for forty-eight hours and is indigestible. The only reason Belle gets at least one date from my clients is because her photos are smoking hot, and she's appeared in the pages of *Maxim*.

Don't make your diet an issue. If you don't see something you can eat on the menu, smoothly ask the server if they have any entrées that meet your specific needs. Just because your date has different eating habits than you, it does not mean he's inferior, and you don't want to make him feel that way. You also don't want to make him feel as if you're easily offended and impossible to please.

CELEBRITIES: Many girls read the tabloids and the latest gossip blogs like men read the *Wall Street Journal*. Believe me, I know. I watch all the infotainment shows, and I buy at least four entertainment publications each week. I use the excuse that I'm looking for mentions of romance, dating, and matchmaking, in case I'm called upon to give a quote about a certain celebrity situation, which I'm often asked to do. But that doesn't stop men's eyes from rolling back in their heads when I start to talk about what I've read. Men might find a little celebrity gossip to be amusing, but when you start talking about movie stars' relationships, styles, and exploits as if they were your own family members, a man's attention will wane, and you'll give him the impression that you spend too much time on frivolous matters, which you probably do.

BUSINESS: Don't lead with your business foot—he's probably exhausted from being at work all day and wants to get away from it. He wants to detox as much as you do. Both your professions are going to come up in conversation, but a critical mistake that most women make is to talk about their degrees, hot business prospects, and their career goals at the very beginning of the conversation. Those of us who have grown up from the '60s on have been taught to talk about our accomplishments, but unfortunately this has left us standing alone at the altar. This is because men do not want to compete in the bedroom like they do in the boardroom. These topics send off masculine signals and immediately desexualize you. I could share story after story about girls in my club who have led with this foot, and as beautiful and intelligent as they are, the men refuse to take the relationship to the next level. The reason is simple: IT'S NOT SEXY!

For example, Lena, a member of The Millionaires' Club, is a tall, sultry, blond, Michelle Pfeiffer lookalike lawyer. She's thirty-three and has already become a partner at one of the top ten firms in LA. But it's often hard for her to get past the initial phone call because she's often using legalese, as if she's depositioning her potential mates before they even meet. My clients call me and say, "I know she's beautiful in her pictures, but I don't know . . . she's so businesslike and masculine." I push the clients on the date and tell them, "Trust me, she's worth going out with." Because of my reputation they listen to me, and they set up a dinner. It's the same story every time.

She gets into the car looking drop-dead gorgeous, and the guy smiles. But his smile fades the minute she opens her mouth and says, "Did you know I went to Stanford and graduated first in my class? Did you know I have multiple degrees? I was going to be a doctor and graduated pre-med, then I got an MBA and switched to law. I was the youngest partner at my firm, and I own my own house in Beverly Hills!" And before he can hit the limp-biscuit button, I get the 911 phone call from the bathroom, "Patti, what have you done to me?" I'm still coaching Lena today, but she refuses to switch her dating demeanor and shut off her left brain for a few seconds. She says she wants a man to love her just the way she is. Unfortunately that hasn't worked for her yet.

So, those are the topics you don't want to talk about on a date. That leaves the rest of the world wide open. There are plenty of other subjects to talk about: sports, travel, literature, culture, movies, nature, your community, music, humor, pets, the media, local and national news—the list goes on and on. You'll get extra points if you do a little research on your date and his interests beforehand. I always have a few girls in my club who pump me for information on their date's interests before they go out. If he works on Wall Street they might not become experts on the stock market, but at least they can ask intelligent questions and recognize some of the terms he's using. The men especially fall head over heels if the girl has knowledge about and interest in their favorite charities and causes. It will come as no surprise that these girls are the most popular ones in the club and date more than anyone else. As a matter of fact, I'm always having to replace them, because my clients take them off the market quickly.

Cool Speak

This is another way your mouth can get you into trouble. I don't know what's wrong with the female members of my club lately, but making idiotic statements they think sound "cool" has been responsible for mucking up more relationships in the very beginning than just about anything else I can think of. When I ask my male members why they don't want a second date with the girls I've introduced them to, it's often because she said one asinine thing that completely turned him off. Here are some examples of Cool Speak.

"I can't believe how much I've been dating lately! I've had a date every night this past week."
"My ex-boyfriend is still really into me, but he's just got to get over it. I mean, I'm ready to move on, so why isn't he?"
"I've never been dumped. I'm always the first to leave."
"It's hard for any one man to keep my attention for very long. I usually get bored and bail after the third date."
"You're the first man I've ever dated under six feet. I've always dated really tall guys."
"I'm a free spirit. I just can't seem to settle down, whether it's with a job or a man."
"I really dressed up tonight. I never look this good nor-

mally. I made an exception for you. I usually run around the house in baggy sweats with dirty hair."

"I can't believe I've had to resort to the internet for a date." (When she's meeting someone she met on the internet.)

"I hate this restaurant. The only reason I come here is to meet single guys."

Warning: Your mouth isn't the only one that can get you in trouble. His mouth can get you in even worse. How? I believe that **men fall in love through their eyes, and women fall in love through their ears.** A man can look at a girl and fall in love, but a woman has to hear his voice and listen to the things he says. A woman can fall in love with a man who has a sexy voice and uses it to seduce her.

A Pair and a Spare

No matter how sparkling a conversationalist you happen to be, no matter how sexy his voice is, chances are you won't meet your perfect match on your first date. You'll have to try on quite a few pairs of shoes before you find the perfect fit. This is a good thing. You'd never dream of buying the first pair of shoes you try, wearing it until it starts hurting you, then buying the next pair you try, would you? You need to try on several pairs, walk around in them for a bit, and see how they compare to each other. Make a firm commitment to yourself that you will not settle down into a relationship with the first guy that asks you out after Dating Detox. My advice to you is that when you first start dating again, always keep a "pair and a spare" handy. I first heard about this from my matchmaking grandmother, believe it or not, and it's never failed anyone who's implemented it.

If you have a Pair and a Spare, it means there are three important men in your life, none of whom are related to you.

1. Best Straight Guy Friend: This is not the guy who's been your best friend for years. He is Harry, from *When Harry Met Sally*. He's the guy you went on a few dates with, didn't feel the spark, but really liked, and so you became great friends. This is the spare: he's the one you can tell all your troubles to, and he'll give you the male perspective. He's the one who will go shopping with you and tell you what really turns a guy on. He's also the guy you can go out with and be seen with in public, just in case another man in your life has gotten the impression you're getting too invested too quickly. It's his number you dial when you're drunk, rather than the number of the guy you're really interested in. He's the consummate escort when you don't have anyone else to go out with, and the one you can take to your cousin's wedding. He's a great friend, and you don't need to feel bad about "using" him. Chances are, you're playing a similar role in his life. And it's not impossible for him to have a wee bit of a crush on you. You might find that when he wipes your dating disaster tears away, that you see him in a new, lovely light, and he could well be the one you end up with after all. There are worse things in life than marrying your best friend. Don't rule him out completely.

2. The Big Maybe: This is the first half of the pair. He's a member of your ten Must-Haves club. He's a "cusper," and you can go either way with him. He's usually your second choice, but don't tell him that. You're not quite ready to put him in the friend category yet. You might see him once a week, and he calls you once or twice a week in between just to chat or check in. He may be dating other people, just like you are, but he clearly wants you. He gives you your space, initiates all dates, and will rearrange his schedule for you. One thing is for sure, he has ambition, and will definitely achieve the goals you desire. That's the reason why most women marry this guy. He's someone with whom it's just too early to tell, and you're taking your time. He is a critical factor in your dating equation, because he helps you to keep your head on straight and not do anything rash or foolish when you meet The One You Really Like.

3. The One You Really Like: This is the man you are instantly, passionately, insanely attracted to. He's the one you can't wait to sleep with, and the one who ignites irrational jealousy when he so much as smiles at the waitress. You feel that he's so perfect for you you're tempted to cruise by his house with your girlfriends, and you conceal your number while dialing his house twelve times a day just to hear his voice on the answering machine. Since this could be the real deal, your perfect match, this is the one you could easily lose your head over and completely alienate in the first month, if you don't have the Big Maybe and Best Straight Guy Friend helping you keep things in perspective. They've got your back and your front, and they keep you in mental line. And if you're keeping yourself occupied with interesting, thoughtful people—people who make you laugh and build your confidence, you'll be happier and more interesting by way of association. You'll be calmer and less inclined to become unnerved by that pins and needles sensation you get when you have a wild crush on someone. The other two keep you happily occupied, so you don't count the hours, minutes, and seconds in between this one's phone calls, and make it impossible for you to focus too intensely on one person.

You know what they say about putting all your eggs in one basket . . . you might be tempted to never even look at another basket ever again, but this is a terribly bad strategy. No relationship needs that kind of pressure in the very beginning. You might be tempted to drop everything when he calls you at 5:00 PM on Saturday evening and asks you out for that night, but because you have a date with The Big Maybe, you have to decline that invitation by saying you already have plans. The One You Really Like could easily be jealous once he finds out about the other two, but if he's smart (and why would you want to date anyone who wasn't?) he'll realize that the other two were a huge asset to both of you when your relationship was just getting off the ground.

Now, it's not always easy to constantly keep a Pair and a Spare in rotation. There will be times when you only have two out of three in your life, sometimes only one, and on occasion, none of the above. Don't lose heart because of this. It's important to get out there and keep on trying. Even if you go out on a date with someone and find that he has no potential whatsoever, you're still getting dating practice in, and everyone needs practice, whether you're eighteen or eighty. You need that practice to feel confident, secure, and at ease. The more you practice, the faster you'll get to the point where the dating process is completely comfortable and effortless. So many men never reach that point, and if you can put them at ease, they will be eternally grateful and attracted to you. The worst is when two insecure people go out, and they both spend so much time trying to build their own confidence that they have little energy left to find out about the other person. At least one of you on the date needs to be cool and calm, and wouldn't you prefer to be that person?

Training the One You Really Like

You're now dating, and you've got an edge with The One You Really Like. If you're on the right relationship road, he'll start by asking you out once a week, then will graduate to two, then three nights, then full weekends, and then monogamy. If he only asks you out on weeknights and hasn't yet set a date for Saturday night, which is prime date night, don't get your panties in a twist just yet. Let's decipher the dating code he's using. Monday through Thursday are only opening, first date nights. You're being fit into his schedule and he's not yet ready to risk a weekend night on you. Friday nights mean you've made it into his number two position, but he's still dating or looking for someone else on Saturday. If he asks you out for Saturday, you are in the prime princess position. Marriage-minded men know that Saturday is the best night of the week to date, because beforehand they can sleep in, hit the gym or golf course with their buddies, and have plenty of time to primp in a manly way. Plus, it allows them to sleep over with you or take you to brunch on Sunday.

What do you do if he has now asked you out for the third Thursday in a row and you desperately want him to ask you out for Saturday night? You're thinking, "Why date me at all if you're not going to give me Saturday?" Remember to be happy, perky, and upbeat. Never sound petulant. Here's the dialogue:

Him: Hi honey! I really want to try that new Thai restaurant that opened up on Clark Street. How about I book us a table for Thursday night? I'll pick you up at seven o'clock.

You: Oh! I heard about that place. I'd love to go, but I already have plans Thursday. (Do not tell him your plans, even if he puts you on the waterboard—you want to maintain a veil of mystery.)

Silence.

Him: No problem, what about Friday?

You: Oh darn! I have plans that night too!

Him: Okay, how about Sunday? I'll pick you up after you go to the gym!

You: Actually the best night for me is Monday night. Can't wait to see you! (Monday night is laundry night for most men. He now clearly gets the message that he's in the dating doghouse.)

At this point, if he really likes you, he will say, "What about Saturday night?" If he doesn't and skips to another day, like brunch on Sunday, tell him this week is just not good for you and banish him for the week. If he has totally annoyed you and you have no hope for this relationship, but you're the type of girl who's a straight shooter, tell him in the sweetest voice you can possibly muster: "I have to be honest with you. I'm looking for a Saturday night guy, and I don't get the sense we're on the same page. But that's okay, because I had a lot of fun with you and I wish you best of luck in your search." You've just completed the gentle kiss-off and your power remains intact.

It's Your Call (Or Is It?)

The phone can be your best friend, or your worst enemy. I think inappropriate phone behavior sabotages more budding relationships than just about anything else, and the same applies to text messaging. On the other hand, a phone call is certainly the most conventional and effective way of setting up a date, checking in, or communicating when you're not together. So I would say that it's imperative that you use the phone correctly. It could be a stick of dynamite in your hand, or a magic wand that grants all your fondest wishes.

In the embryonic stages of a dating relationship (first

through sixth date) the most important thing to remember about the phone is not to use it too much. Always return his calls promptly (see First Commandment of Dating), but do not initiate any calls. If he says, "Call me," you should quickly say, "I'm a traditional girl. I prefer you to call me."

And when you do talk on the phone, give him fifteen minutes only (use a timer if you have to), then give him an upbeat excuse to get off, such as, "I'm off to the gym," "I have company here," or "I have to walk my dog." Four excuses you should not use: business, laundry, your favorite TV show, or your need to call your mother.

Your reasons for wanting him to call you, instead of vice versa, are twofold:

1. Men and women feel differently about phone calls. For the most part, a man uses his phone for business, whether it's the business of setting up a meeting, buying or selling stock, or making a date. To a woman, the phone is a social tool. We use it to chat, share our feelings, hear each other's voices, and relate on a very personal level. If you call him when he's in business mode and you're in social mode, you are both going to be frustrated. You never want to be seen as an interruption or a burden, and you have no way of knowing when he's really ready to speak to you unless he calls you. When a man calls you, that's a good sign. A smart man knows that a woman falls in love between her ears and realizes it's crucial for you to hear his voice in order for him to charm you. If he's a texter/emailer,

you may not fall in love with him, because he's showing signs that he's impersonal.

This all changes, of course, when you're in a committed relationship. At that point, you have the right
to check in via phone and call him when you need
him. But even then, you should only give him one
check-in call for every three check-in calls he makes
to you. The same goes for texting.

2. He who calls more has the most interest, and the least
control. Once again I'm telling you, let HIM call YOU.
If you were in the middle of a business deal, would
you hound the buyer with phone calls, constantly asking how he was feeling, when you would be seeing
him again, etc.? I think not! Simply put, calling a man
more than he calls you means you like him more than
he likes you, and you've lost your power. Do you want
to be perceived as needy or demanding? In this man
market with so much competition from other beautiful women, you want to be a mystery, and let him be
intrigued by you. Think of it as a poker game. She who
doesn't show her hand has the power. **Give him space
to chase**, my friend. You'll both appreciate it.

One of my closest friends found out the wisdom in my
phone rules firsthand, but in a way you'd never suspect. Sandy
is gorgeous and well educated, although not the brightest
when it comes to dating. She'd made her share of mistakes
when trying to lead men, being too aggressive, and simply
talking too much. I advised her that her relationships would

be much more successful if she would just sit still, smell good, and shut up—let the man take the lead. It's not that women should be seen and not heard, it's just that she needed to give him room to feel like a man.

She met a strapping, sexy, successful guy with whom she had many things in common: both had parents who were working professionals, both were self-made, and they even lived in the same neighborhood in New York (where that can be all important). The first date was heaven for them both— he picked her up, took her to her favorite restaurant, they laughed, held hands, looked deeply into each other's eyes, and she saw a future there. She wasn't too worried when at the end of the date, he said, "Call me." She intended to follow my advice about not calling, but she was confident she'd hear from him soon. It took him an entire week to call her again, however, and make another date, which is not a good sign. At this point Sandy should have gone back to her Pair and a Spare. But instead she obsessed over The One She Really Likes.

The second date was not as extravagant—dinner in a casual restaurant and a movie. There wasn't as much interaction, but apparently there was enough for him to try to sleep with her at the end of the date. She sweetly but firmly told him that she wasn't the kind of girl who would have sex with someone unless she felt safely and securely committed in a monogamous relationship. But she didn't stop there. Again the director came out—she told him she didn't think either one of them was ready for that yet. He disappeared.

Two weeks later she received a call from him. Seething, he didn't even bother to ask her if it was a good time to talk, how her day was. Instead, he got straight to his poison-tipped point. "How come you never call me?" he thundered. "What's wrong with you?"

Keeping her cool, she told him, "You have every right to feel the way you do, and I'm sorry you're upset." But then, annoyed that he'd taken two weeks to call, she couldn't maintain her calm and abruptly said, "I don't call men!" It would have been better for her to say sweetly, "I'm just an old-fashioned girl who feels uncomfortable calling a man that I'm not in a relationship with yet, for fear that I might call you and you might have another woman there." By saying this you've stated your vulnerability and your innocence, which is exactly what a man wants.

"So you won't sleep with me unless we're in an established relationship, and you won't call me unless we're in a relationship, for God's sake, woman, you have too many rules! You are way too high maintenance for me. See ya!"

Instead of cursing me for the advice I gave her, Sandy thanked me, and I'll tell you why. This guy revealed the unflattering truth about himself in the very beginning, which is the best time to find out. He was not a hunter in search of a wife, full of masculine energy and a hard cock. He was a limp, lazy loser, oozing feminine energy and lethargy. Yes, he came on to her after the second date, but that showed he wasn't really willing to work for her. He wanted to go the lazy route and slip right in, without going through the rigors of courtship. Instead of being appreciative of her being mindful of his schedule and his privacy, he wanted her to call him, to chase him, to do all the work. Ladies, if he's like that in the beginning, he'll take forever to commit to you, and if he ever does, be prepared to do all the work in the marriage. There will be no safe harbor for you with him—you will be exhausted for the rest of your life, and he'll turn into your son, not your husband. And believe me, the divorce will cost you.

The phone turned out to be her magic wand, stripping the handsome prince of his looks and revealing him for the slacker that he was. I rest my case.

The Ten Commandments of Dating

Every female who joins the Millionaire's Club gets a copy of my Ten Commandments of Dating. Men get twice as many commandments as women because they're not fast learners. Ninety-nine times out of one hundred, when someone comes crying to me about their relationship, it's because one or the other has broken one of the commandments. Getting the relationship back on track is simply a matter of deciding which one was broken and figuring out how to fix it. I've rewritten my Ten Commandments of Dating so they're more general and less Millionaire's Club–specific for you. No matter your age, race, or religion, they are set in stone just like the ones Moses received on Mount Sinai, and you break them at your own peril. Note: I've already mentioned some of these rules but they're so important that I give myself a free pass to drill them into you again. It will also be helpful for you to have all the big no-no's in one place. In fact, go ahead and dog-ear this page now for easy reference in the future.

1. THOU SHALT RETURN CALLS PROMPTLY. Return a potential's call within twenty-four to forty-eight hours on weekdays, or seventy-two hours on weekends or holidays. Forget whatever Rules you've read, busy men get perturbed if they don't hear back from you within that time frame. It's best to call them back immediately, as men today have so many choices when it comes to dating, and if you don't call him back sooner rather then later, he'll dial his next option. Plus, it's just plain rude not to return a call promptly, whether it's business or personal. If you don't, a man who's looking for a real relationship will feel you're playing games or are just too busy for him. He'll lose interest and move on to another woman—nobody's getting any younger here!

By the same token, expect your potential match to return your return calls promptly, but if he doesn't, don't make a big deal of it. If you get a message from him that he's trying to reach you, call him back only once on his cell phone. Mirror him. If he texts you, text him back. Don't complain about it or scold him.

2. THOU SHALT HONOR THY DATING COMMITMENTS. Nobody likes a flake. When a man you think you might be interested in musters up the courage to ask you out (and believe me, it never gets any easier for a guy, no matter how experienced he is), you must make a plan with him and stick to it. I don't care if Lance Armstrong calls later and asks you out

for the same night—Lance will find you more intriguing if
you're not so readily available. Even if you have the distinct
feeling the guy you already have plans with is not going to
be the answer to your prayers, be gracious and attentive to
him. If his company is so disagreeable to you, you never should
have accepted the date in the first place. Remember, you're
gathering experience for Dating Data, and cultivating a Pair
and a Spare. Always consider your word to be golden and
your commitments unbreakable. This is important for building your own self-respect, as well as gaining the respect of
others.

Note: if you meet a man who doesn't honor his dating
commitments and is a double booker or best-offer boy, then
he is not worth your time, love, or patience.

3. THOU SHALT LET THE MAN TAKE THE LEAD. Let
him call you first. Let him ask you out. If he's shy, feel free to
invite him to a party or a group event, but let him be the one
to make the first move and suggest the first date. Nothing
makes a man feel better about himself than working for and
winning what he considers to be the grand prize, so don't rob
him of the pleasure by turning the tables and chasing him.
Let him feel he's cleverly tracking you by suggesting where
and when your first several dates will happen. You may make
suggestions (to build up Dating Data) but don't direct him. If
you do the initiating in the beginning, you'll set the precedent
for life, and you'll have to do all the initiating in the future.
What woman wants to have to instigate everything? If you
want to be romanced, let the man lead—there's no way

around that. If you don't let the man lead, you'll turn him into a couch potato.

4. IN THE BEGINNING, THOU SHALT LEAVE THE PAST IN THE PAST. Any talk of old boyfriends or girlfriends is strictly taboo at first (and forever, if you can get away with it.) Men can't help it—they will picture you naked and having sex with some other guy, and they'd really rather not go there. Most want to believe that they're the only one who could ever truly satisfy you. You might think you're being very clever and showing off your rapier wit tossing out all your "hilarious" dating disaster stories, but your guy can't help but think, "Okay, there must be something wrong with her to have dated so many losers." In the same vein, don't unpack all your baggage too soon. Deep, personal history is simply too much intimate information for either one of you to process in the beginning—save your deep, dark secrets for at least six months down the road when you're in a committed relationship and you know you can trust him. We all have skeletons in our closets. The man you're dating will have his share as well. But they should come out naturally, in their time, after you've fallen in love with each other and you're willing to deal with each other's messes.

5. THOU SHALT BE ENGAGING. Focus your attention on him—don't let your eyes or interest wander, even if the waiter has the most adorable butt you've ever seen. Answer his questions with positive energy and enthusiasm. If witty banter is not your forte, at least ask interesting questions. Be a good listener, with full eye contact—let him look into those baby blues, big browns, or gorgeous greens and make sure you gaze into his. Also, make sure you get a word or two in edgewise, so he gets to know a little about you as well. A good conversation is like a ping-pong match, with the ball bouncing back and forth and both people scoring points. But a wise woman lets the man take the lead in handing out personal information or revealing himself. Remember, knowledge is power—it's helpful to know more about him than he does about you. She who has the most knowledge has the most power. He'll never realize you're banking information—he'll just feel like you know him really well and find him fascinating—two things men crave in a woman. A great tip is for every three questions he asks you, ask one back. If you let the man lead the conversation and give him home-court advantage, his chest will puff up, and other organs too! If you talk fifty-fifty, it will neutralize the sex factor, and if you talk more than he does, he'll go to sleep.

6. THOU SHALT NOT DRINK TOO MUCH ON A DATE.
Although you might be tempted to throw several back in an effort to relax, or maybe he's plying you with really great wine, you want to stay clear and focused at all times. Usually more than two drinks will cloud a girl's judgment. Drunk and sloppy is never attractive, and you don't want to get into a situation that is beyond your control. There will be far fewer regrets if you're fully cognizant throughout your encounter. Besides, if it's a really great date, you'll want to remember every second of it. Men can usually hold their liquor better than women

and can often drink more than two drinks without getting tipsy. Be conscious of how much he drinks, and be on the lookout for alcoholics—they're often the drinkers at dinner and not the eaters. A real man will share a bottle of wine but won't mix it with hard liquor, unless it's a ten-course meal.

7. THOU SHALT NOT BE A GOLD DIGGER. Don't you dare ask or hint for anything of monetary value! If he offers to buy you something without so much as a hint from you, go ahead and accept it, but make sure there are no strings attached, and be ready to give it back if he starts trying to pull those strings. If he offers you cash, however, never, I repeat, NEVER accept it. Sometimes a generous guy will offer to pay your credit card balance or your rent for the month, but don't let him do it—ever. Deep down inside, he'll feel like he's buying your affection, and you'll owe him that and more. Besides, what do we call women who accept money from men? That's right, baby. Ho ho ho. The exception to this rule is when you're in a monogamous, committed relationship and on the road to marriage, and he asks you to go away on a trip with him, and you can't afford to go because you need to work to pay your rent. If he offers to pay your rent under those conditions, it's fine to accept it.

This is very important: you are NOT considered a gold digger if you expect him to pay for the dates. If he expects you to pay or split the check or talks about moving in together and splitting the rent ("We should live together, it will be cheaper"), he does not have signs of a providership, which means he will not be a good husband.

8. THOU SHALT ACT LIKE A LADY. No cussin', no scratchin', no sittin' with your legs spread wide. This might sound obvious, but you should hear some of the stories my male clients tell me. Most men want their women to be refined and don't want to hear a stream of f-words spewing from their lips. Just ask my ex-boyfriend, who constantly elbowed me every time I cussed. So I'm not perfect.

Acting like a lady also involves being polite and following common laws of courtesy, such as saying "please," "thank you," and "excuse me." You must also be prompt and not make him wait more than ten minutes for you. Why some women feel they can keep a man waiting while they do their hair and makeup is beyond me. That gives the man the impression that you don't care about his time schedule and that you're only concerned about your own. He'll also think you spend far too much time primping, and he'll look for someone else who is more natural and spontaneous. Part of acting like a lady involves allowing him to be a gentleman. Let him open doors for you, help you with your coat, even order your meal for you. It will make him feel like a manly man who is gracious and in control of the situation. Men yearn to feel that way. Throw him a bone. It won't kill you.

CAUTION: You should always thank a man for the date while you're on it—that's sufficient. But NEVER call or text him to say thank you the day after. Remember, **women fall in love on the date, and men fall in love after the date.** If you contact him the next day because he spent so much money on you that you feel guilty, you've now disrupted his process period, and he will lose the connection with you.

9. THOU SHALT EXPRESS SINCERE INTEREST AND APPRECIATION. Men like genuine compliments just as much as you do (maybe even more) so don't be afraid to tell him he's handsome, interesting, or funny. Don't go overboard, of course, by offering to clean his bathroom after the first date, but once you've decided you like a guy and he's taken you out several times, it's important to show your appreciation and reciprocate—follow the 4:1 Rule: once he takes you out four times, do something nice for him, like making him dinner at your place. Oh, how men love a home-cooked meal!

10. THOU SHALT NOT BECOME INTIMATE ON THE FIRST DATE. If you're interested in him, there's nothing wrong with a little nookie—and by that I mean hugs and kisses. But if this one has keeper potential, it's best to take it slow and get to know him first, for at least three months, or until, in the sober light of day, he suggests a monogamous relationship. How many times have you heard that desperate: "But of course you're the only one!" while he's frantically fumbling with your bra after one too many margaritas? Whatever you do, don't assume you're monogamous just because you're seeing a lot of each other. Until you have The Conversation about exclusivity, just assume he's going out with other women. And by the way, as long as you are not exclusive, you have the right to date as many other men as you want. I advise you to exercise that right. Also, don't think you can get around this rule with a blow job. In my estimation, in is in. It's all sex to me—and to him.

When a man wants to have sex with you and he has a few pennies in his pocket, he will often suggest a weekend away. It can be anything from the Best Western to the Four Seasons, but it's still a weekend away. Under no circumstances are you allowed to go away for the weekend unless he gets you a hotel room for yourself. The conversation should go like this:

GUY SAYS: I'm having such a great time with you, I would love to take you to Santa Barbara for the weekend.

GIRL SAYS: I would love to go to Santa Barbara. That's my favorite place in the whole world, however, I need to be clear about something: I'm not the type of girl who sleeps around, and I certainly don't want to give you that impression. Since we're not in a monogamous, committed relationship, I would need to have my own hotel room.

GUY SAYS: (Nothing—complete silence.)

GIRL SAYS: (Nothing—complete silence. Do not make a sound. Hold your breath if you have to. **Men don't respond to talk, they respond to silence.**)

Awkward pause continues. Guy is processing.

If the guy wants that exclusive, monogamous relationship, he'll ask for it. Negotiations are in play. If it's a new relationship and he's got major money and is qualifying you but still respects you, he'll get you your own room (with an adjoining door). In any case, you've retained your power and your purity.

11. THOU SHALT NOT WEAR TOO MUCH BLING. Okay, there really isn't an eleventh commandment. I just like to throw this in for the fun of it. If you wear too much jewelry on your dates, he won't have anything to buy you!

As much fun as your Adventures in Dating may be, remember the object of all these new experiences and excitement is to find your perfect match. You're not practicing catch and release here just for the sport of it. You might find yourself enjoying so many dating options you don't know which one to choose. If you can't make a decision about which one you should focus on, it's probably because none of the men you're seeing is quite right, and you're not ready to settle down just yet. But don't worry. Your heart will tell you when you've found the guy who will take your hand and lead you into the next step, the First Days of Infatuation.

STEP SIX

First Days of Infatuation

I n the beginning when you and your guy meet and start dating, the first ninety days are both exquisitely joyful, and excruciatingly painful. You feel like you're trying to walk a tightrope while drunk. Infatuation and hormones are racing like the Grand Prix, yet you must very carefully negotiate the all-important sexual, social, and emotional minefields of a brand-new relationship. While your pulse is thumping and your heart is doing backflips, you have to attempt to calmly and objectively figure out the answers to important questions like: How do I know if he's a keeper? When do we have sex? How often do we see each other? What roles do we play in each other's lives?

These are difficult things to be objective about when you're so smitten with each other you can't see straight, and every little habit, even the gross, annoying ones like burping after meals and leaving the bathroom door open, seem endearing. On the other hand, you could just as easily catch a glimpse of his true, clashing colors during the first ninety days, decide that he's not worth one more second of your invaluable time, and set him free for someone else to deal with.

The goal of the first ninety days is to either become involved in an exclusive relationship or to decide that he is absolutely not The One. The first ninety days should be easier for you than they are for him, because he's the one who is supposed to do most of the work. It's all so much easier when you embrace the fact that all you need to do is smell good, look good, sit back, and relax.

But don't take it too easy during this phase of your relationship. If you make the mistake of being inattentive to him just because it's new, you'll never get the chance to grow old together. Provided you think he has potential, don't be too difficult with availability or timing, or he'll think you're not interested.

One of the major complaints I get from my male clients is, "She doesn't have time for me!" Granted, my wealthy clients are a lot more demanding than your average Joe, but it's true that there are countless women out there who put their jobs, schooling, friends, or family first. We do it as a defense mechanism—it's far easier to control these parts of our lives than our love lives. At work, you push certain buttons, you get certain results. But in love, the other person is a completely random variable over which we have absolutely no control. At least that's the way it feels during the first ninety days. Trust that you will learn how to control without directing. But in the meantime, know that **if you don't put your man first, you'll end up last**. If you make yourself too busy with other things, you shouldn't be dating—you're not looking for a serious partner, you're looking for an occasional playmate.

Usually, during the first ninety days of infatuation, finding enough time for him is not an issue. You're inclined to want to be around him 24-7, but you know that's impossible and unhealthy. When you're in the midst of the blissful turmoil of the first ninety days, it will help to gain a little perspective of what's ahead. Time frames vary, but generally there are four phases of a relationship, and each one lasts about ninety days. In my opinion, if you really want marriage, once you've gone through these four phases in one year and you're still not engaged, it's time to pick up and move on. Now, if you're young, maybe eighteen to twenty-two years old, you have up to two years for this, but you will need at least a promise ring, if he can't afford an engagement ring. In the meantime, to maintain some perspective during the first-ninety-day crazies, here are the:

FOUR PHASES OF A RELATIONSHIP

1. Honeymoon. Don't take this literally—you are not to schtup like bunnies during the first three months. This is the time when you meet each other, decide you're attracted, and begin exploring what a monogamous relationship would be like together. If the attraction is shallow, one of the two of you will disappear. If the attraction is deep, you will look at each other through a soft-focus lens and believe everything is perfect. During this phase, the man is Sir Galahad. As in my ex-boyfriend's case, he'll drive an hour to get to your house kill a black widow spider for you. This is the flowers and champagne stage, when he's trying to impress you with grandiose dates and major effort. His deeds don't have to include spending money, but they're always backed up by thought and consideration. Enjoy this phase when you're in it, because it usually doesn't last beyond ninety days.

2. Discern and Decide. Now that you've settled down into a monogamous relationship, the blinders are off and the hormones have cooled a bit, you start looking at each other more objectively, and you're better able to decide if he is someone who could make you happy in the long run. This is when the yuckie comes out, and it's the easiest time to end a relationship.

3. Negotiation to Engagement: So he passed the first six months, now you begin to decide whether you want to spend the rest of your life with him. You can start wondering about, and experimenting with, building a life together. This is when you share your deep, dark secrets and decide if you can deal with each other's messes. This should also be when you start spending quality time with each other's families, if you haven't already. After eight to nine months together, it's time to pish or get off the pot, as my Yiddish grandmother would say. A proposal, or at least serious talk of one, should be forthcoming.

4. Engagement. If you think you're home free just because he popped the question, guess again. Work on your relationship begins in earnest now, because you're unequivocally playing for keeps. Even if you're madly in love and getting along splendidly, you might consider relationship counseling during this phase, just to make sure you have realistic expectations and that healthy boundaries are established. You'll be surprised by how much you, and your love, grow during this phase.

During the Honeymoon phase, it's really difficult to be objective. You see the object of your desire as flawless, and you can't wait for the time when you can actually call him your boyfriend. And once you do, you start inserting him in all your conversations: "My *boyfriend* says . . ." "Can I bring my *boyfriend?*" "My *boyfriend* was just telling me about . . ." "Let me check with my *boyfriend*." He's a status symbol and you want to show him off like an Hermès Birkin bag, and you can't wait to introduce him to your friends (although they're getting sick of hearing about him already). Regardless of this mini-obsession, you need to keep in mind that there are **Three C's of a Relationship:**

Chemistry. Does he make your heart pound and your toes curl? When you're alone in bed at night, do you replay all his tender touches, the words he used to make your heart melt? At the end of a date, do you want to rip his pants off and have your way with him right there on the doorstep? If, however, you don't feel this way yet, don't worry. Remember, **women are like Crock-Pots, they heat up slowly, and men are like microwaves, instantly ready to go.** As long as you think he's cute and you have fun with him, he's a contender.

Compatibility. How do you "roll" together? Are you comfortable with silence? Do you feel constant pressure to prove yourself to him, or does he make you feel like you're perfect the way you are? Do you "get" each other? How do your energy levels match up? Do you love/hate the same things? Compatibility basically means that your routines mesh, you enjoy doing the same things, and you want the same things at the same time. For example, if you want kids and he doesn't, you are NOT compatible.

Communication. Do you feel you can tell him anything, or do you have to watch what you say around him? How do you each express your emotions, wants, and needs, and are you comfortable talking about them? How do you argue? How do you settle disagreements? It's not an issue of whether or not you have a difference of opinion, what's important is how you resolve those differences. Consideration is the key to communication, because if you feel cherished, you'll reward him with respect, and like Verizon, no one will ever have to ask, "Can you hear me now?"

To be honest, you're lucky if he meets 51 percent, even a fraction more than half, of your needs in the Three C's. Diversity in a relationship is good and healthy—it means you can each learn from the other. How boring would it be if your mate were exactly like you? It's our differences that make us interesting, and often attract us to each other. Besides, he's a man. He's wired differently. He's never going to be exactly like you. The Three C's are simply something to consider during the first ninety days, in between the times you're talking about him and dreaming about him.

The Space Brace

The Pair and a Spare will be your salvation during this precarious time—they will divert you. It is crucial that you not obsess about him, and if you can't help yourself, at least don't let him see it. You both need what I call a Space Brace during the first ninety days. You might be tempted to call each other constantly and slop mushy terms of endearment into every other sentence, but you need a little space to brace a secure relationship. You don't need to know what he's doing every night, so don't ask. You both need to continue seeing your friends. If he wants a boys' night out, encourage him, and organize a girls' night. Resist the urge to check up on him. Don't cruise his house or office. Keep a safe distance, and make sure he keeps his.

Also, don't keep checking his Facebook or MySpace page. And stop analyzing the snapshots of him with other women on his personal page. One of my assistants is always doing that, and it drives me crazy. She looks at the MySpace page of her current guy and analyzes the pictures, saying things like, "I can tell he's really into her by the smile on his face," or "Look at all the girls in his pictures. He would never date me; I'm a blonde." Remember, he put those pictures up before he even met you. And please don't ask him questions about the girls in the photos. "Who's the one on the left? How did you meet her?" FYI, he's doing the same thing to your personal page, so be damn careful what you put up. If you've posted photos of yourself being sloppy or risqué (*Girls Gone Wild* photos), or if you're a celebrity whore and you have pictures of your favorite celebrities, or if you put the classic photo up where you're gazing adoringly at your ex-boyfriend, that will sink the ship before it even leaves the port.

Above all, DO NOT MOVE IN WITH HIM DURING THE FIRST NINETY DAYS OF INFATUATION. As a matter of fact, I don't think you should move in with your intended until you have an engagement ring, a wedding date, and your parents have met. Your own living accommodations are the ultimate Space Brace. Absence makes the heart grow fonder, you know. Besides, why would a guy buy the house if he can live there rent free? In other words, why should he marry you if he can have all the benefits of matrimony without making any investment? Still not convinced? I'll go more deeply into this in Step Seven.

I know we've all seen it in the movies many times, and we've probably all heard it happen to a friend of ours: "We fell madly in love and knew this was *it* on our first date. It was a Friday. We spent the entire weekend together, and by Sunday night he'd packed his things and moved into my apartment." I don't care if his lease is up or he's getting kicked off his best friend's couch and has no place else to go. I don't care if your roommate just moved out and you're not sure how you're going to pay next month's rent. You desperately need some space to objectively evaluate his pros and cons and to recognize the danger signs. "Danger, Will Robinson!" If he's already living with you, you tend to ignore them—sometimes until it's too late.

Danger Signs

1. Cagey About Calls: If he's only given you a cell or office number and never calls you from home, dump him—he's married. This also applies to the guy who only texts or emails. He may write you long emails, but he'll never call you because he doesn't want his wife to hear your conversation.

2. Excessive Spontaneity: If he only calls you out of the blue and shows up at your doorstep expecting you to go somewhere with him right then and there, he is not spontaneous, he is acting like the boy next door, and will never grow up. You don't have time for that kind of childishness. He's definitely not good husband or father material.

3. Substance Abuse: Be very cautious if it occurs to you that he's drinking an awful lot of wine with dinner after he's already had two Scotches. Or if he opens a bottle of beer the second he gets home from work and goes through an entire six-pack before he goes to bed. Worst of all, be wary if he goes to the bathroom every hour and comes back to you rubbing his nose and sniffling, or with red eyes and a silly grin. He definitely has issues you might not be equipped to deal with. It may make you feel noble to try to help an addict, but let me tell you something: healthy cannot date unhealthy. I don't care how much you love him, you've got to let him solve his problems on his own. You simply cannot be with someone who does not love himself enough to heal himself.

4. Strained Family Relationships: Beware the man who hates his mother or his sister(s). He's not inclined to treat the women in his life well. And if he has issues with his dad, they're definitely going to affect his fathering skills. Many of my clients who don't want children say it's because their own fathers did such an awful job. If you don't want children, that's fine, but if you do, you could be heading down a one-way street to disappointment town.

5. Mommy Issues: There is such a thing as a guy being too close to his family, especially to his mother. If he talks to her several times a day on the phone, and even takes her calls during your date, it's a really bad sign. You will never be good enough for her son, and he will value her opinions above all others, especially yours.

6. Uncontrollable Rage: Does he curse and yell in traffic? Does he use angry, foul language? Does he pound on tables and walls? Does he let other people annoy him to the extent that he gets in verbal or physical altercations? If so, he is not just an aggressive alpha male. He is a jerk. Make him go away, but do it gently, in case his rage turns on you.

7. Dishonesty: This could well be the most common problem of all—pay attention to the little white lies you catch him in, because they usually add up to huge whoppers. He might stretch the truth a bit in order to impress you— claiming he's done things he hasn't, knows people he doesn't, etc. You might be tempted to let him slide, but remember, it's all about integrity. If he's willing to sacrifice his integrity just to impress you, that tells you just how much honesty means to him. A liar is a liar is a liar, no matter how big or small the tales they tell, to you or anyone else. You'll never be able to trust him.

8. Egotism: This could be the second most common problem. Maybe his mother raised him to think he could do no wrong. Or perhaps he has bought into that societal crap that teaches, "Everyone's a winner, no matter what they do!" Or it could mean that he's just always out for himself. Watch him closely: if he takes the best and last portions, walks in front of you, and is overconscious of what people are saying or thinking about him, you will never be number one in his life. That space is reserved for him and him alone.

9. Vanity: They spend so much time working out and grooming themselves that they're far too aware of their own looks and image. It's embarrassing to pass a mirror with them, because they stop and stare at themselves, transfixed. They'll often put other people down, making catty comments about their looks, in order to feel better about themselves. Who needs the competition? Dump him before the third date.

10. Text and Email Obsessed: Calling makes the man, texting makes the boy, email makes the phantom. If your main form of communication when you're not together is texting, it's a sign of immaturity, and he might not be ready for an adult relationship. Real men use the phone. You may think texting is a quicker, more efficient way to communicate, but in reality, it takes less time to dial a number and say a few words than it does to type in a message, no matter how good you are with your thumbs. The man who texts doesn't want to actually speak to you—he's like the kid who just wants to poke you to let you know he's there. By the same token, if he's an excessive emailer, he's more comfortable on-line than in person. He's hiding. He's a phantom.

Now, I'm not saying that you should reject a guy at the slightest hint of any of the aforementioned Danger Signs. No one's perfect, and, as you were reading through the list, you probably found yourself contemplating, "I wonder if I do that?" I know I personally have a little problem with exaggeration when I get overly excited, and I hope it's not perceived as dishonesty—with me it's more for maximum entertainment value. But I digress. I don't think there's a woman out there who hasn't suffered a bad breakup and hasn't said something like, "I should have seen it coming—all the signs were there." I'm just pointing out a few little warning signs that you might want to heed.

On the flip side, my clients are always telling me that there are certain danger signs they look out for in a woman. Their major complaints about women include:

She's flaky
She's needy
She's demanding
She's high maintenance
She wants to live beyond her means
She has a ridiculous sense of entitlement
She's bitter
She's not rational
She doesn't know what she wants
She doesn't make me a priority

She's picky
She's deceitful
She's insecure
She's not feminine enough

And the number one complaint I hear about American women is: SHE DOESN'T COOK! Men LOVE women who cook. Take a class if you don't know how. Buy yourself a cookbook.

The Big O

All the caution in the world, or five thousand Danger Signs glaring in your face won't do you a bit of good if you sleep with him too soon. Premature copulation can hobble your relationship faster than Kathy Bates wielding a mallet. Why? Mostly because of the crazy little hormone I've mentioned before called oxytocin.

The oxytocin that's released, even by touch, let alone intercourse and orgasm, is making you think "OHGODOHGODOHGOD I'VE FOUND MY SOOOOOOOUL MATE!" while he's probably thinking, "I might tap that again."

Oxytocin is what encourages you to let that Bad Boyfriend back into your life because the sex was so good. It's what keeps you involved with the same commitmentphobic slacker for two, three, four years, even though he's never even introduced you to his parents. It's what makes you waste hundreds of hours watching your guy play softball or video games, even though they bore you to tears. It's what makes you overlook "little" indiscretions like serial cheating and STDs, because a guy who gives you screaming orgasms can't be all bad, right?

The diabolical thing about oxytocin is that even if the sex is bad, if you have an orgasm with him, it will still bind you to that lame lover. Just touching, cuddling, and even smelling a masculine odor can increase levels of the little *o* in your body. And get this, girls—when you have repeated orgasms with someone, even the mere *sight* of him can make you release the bonding hormone, making you want to be with him even more. If you don't believe me, google Diane M. Witt, a psychology professor at Binghamton University. Her studies will blow you away.

Men definitely have an advantage over us girls in that they really don't have to worry about oxytocin bonding. All they have to be concerned about is wearing a condom. **Real men wear protection.** We, as women, risk so much more when we have intercourse. Pregnancy is always an issue for those of us in our childbearing years, no matter what type of birth control we may be using. Also, because of the way we're built, we're more susceptible to STDs, AIDS, and even cancer (ain't no man out there who has to worry about the possibility of cervical cancer exacerbated by sex). Men also have no concerns about the biological clock: it wouldn't matter if they spent their thirties and forties under an oxytocin spell with the wrong person, because they don't have time-sensitive ovaries. Many of the lucky dogs can keep on impregnating well into their seventies or even eighties.

What If He Doesn't Go Schwing?

So, it is critically important that you negotiate the whole sex issue with the utmost finesse, and 99.9 percent of the time this will come up during the first ninety days of infatuation. There are, however, a few reasons why it might not come up until later. If the man you're seeing doesn't try to get you in bed during the first ninety days, it could be because of one of the following reasons:

1. **Low testosterone:** There are men out there who are simply asexual—they're just not interested in sex. They really don't care whether they close the deal or not. If you consider yourself to be passion's plaything, then this could be a deal breaker—set him free for the woman who has a low sex drive of her own. She's out there, and these two will relish each other. Or, if you really like and see so many good qualities in him, have patience and faith. He might come around when he feels more secure in the relationship.

2. **Religion:** Those who are saving themselves for marriage are becoming more and more common all the time. While I'm all for sampling the wares before I buy, I'm a firm believer in to each his own, whatever works best for you. I know a lot of devout Christians who adhere to this way of thinking, and they have phenomenal marriages.

3. **Antidepressants:** This is probably the most common reason of all for a man not being interested in sex. So many people are in therapy and on medication these days. I don't think the issue of a low sex drive is as important as the reason

for taking the medication in the first place. You might want to check back in with this one a few miles down the road, when he's in a better emotional place to become involved.

4. Getting his pipes cleaned elsewhere: Every once in a while you'll run across a guy who purports himself to be the perfect gentleman—he says he's in no rush and wants to get to know you better before you sleep together for the first time. There's something a little fishy about him, though—he probably doesn't take you out very consistently. You might find that he has a backup girl waiting in the wings, the booty call who will go over and service him after he leaves you with a chaste kiss at the doorstep.

5. Low self-esteem: This poor, sweet guy simply lacks the confidence to make a move. He can't believe you're even dating him, let alone would want to sleep with him. Don't mistake his lack of ardor for indifference—if he's asking you out regularly, especially every Saturday night, he is way interested. And the good news is that if he doesn't have the confidence to make a move on you, there's no way he's going to be seeing anyone else. Have patience with this guy, and give him lots of encouragement.

6. Sexual ambiguity: This is by far the worst reason of all. He might be using you to prove to himself, his friends, and his family that he's straight, and we all know how well that works. A possible sign of this is an aversion to kissing any part of your body, but especially your mouth, with tongue. He might be very demonstrative in public—he's trying to show the world and himself he's straight. But behind closed doors he won't be able to look you in the eye and press his lips to yours, because it's not the soft, moist, feminine contact he's looking for—it's something hard and scratchy.

You can decide for yourself which of the above reasons are deal breakers. If you're recently out of a very difficult, very physical relationship, you might find solace and comfort with the man who has a slow hand and peter. These men, for the most part, are in the minority.

The Big Exclusivity Talk

The vast majority of men think they deserve a little pokey-pokey by at least the third date. I've prepared a speech for you to use that is really quite comprehensive on the subject. Make sure you memorize it, because you'll find yourself using it often. When passions are high, his hands are wandering, and he's trying to nudge you into the bedroom, you sit up straight, put a little distance between the two of you so that he's thinking with his big head and not the little one, look him straight in the eye and say: "I'm really attracted to you, but I'm not the type of girl who sleeps around. I need to be in an exclusive, committed, monogamous relationship before I can have sex."

You don't negotiate, you don't apologize, you don't scold him, and you don't direct him. You're a boundaries girl, not a bitch. You lay your cards out on the table and wait for him to respond. Do not be a Chatty Cathy and blabber on. Let him have time to process the information and don't interrupt him with more talk.

If you're really lucky and alcohol isn't clouding his judgment, he'll ask for exclusivity right then and there, and say something like, "I'm not sleeping with anybody else—I don't want to sleep with anybody else. You're the only one for me." That's what my stepfather said to my mother, and even though that was many years ago, there are many men out there who feel this way today. That's what distinguishes the men from the boys. A real man is concerned about how and where he spreads his seed.

But even if your guy swears his true love and monogamy on the spot, I still wouldn't advise jumping in the sack right away. He could be talking with his dick, as so many men do, especially when they're turned on. It's very important that you tell him you want to revisit the subject in the sober light of day, then send him home. After that, you must wait for him to bring it up again, preferably not in a fit of passion. You want to make absolutely sure that he is sincere when he commits to you.

In addition, it's very important to discuss each other's physical conditions before jumping into the sack. I'm talking about STDs and AIDS. This can be another good way of cooling things off in the heat of the moment. If you're on the verge of saying, "Oh to hell with it! I need to feel him inside me right now," play a mind game with yourself. Envision his penis . . . covered with crusty, pussy, oozing red sores all over it. Now imagine your vagina in the same condition, because you caught it from him. Imagine yourself running directly to the clinic to get an AIDS test, then agonizing over the results. That will put a damper on things, pronto. These days it isn't safe or smart to have intimate relations without having the big health talk first. If neither one of you has been tested recently, you need to make a pact to each get tested for AIDS and other STDs before you go any further. His willingness to do this is an indication of how sincere he is about having a monogamous relationship with you.

If one of you has herpes, for example, even if it's dormant at the moment, you both need to know if the virus is present and make your decisions accordingly. There can even be legal repercussions from this. If you don't disclose your condition truthfully, he can sue you. Modern medications may be able to keep herpes at bay, but the price someone pays when they contract the virus is having to tell a potential lover about it beforehand, no matter what stage it's in. If you don't know how to explain your condition to him, get some help from your gynecologist. Then you can both make your decisions accordingly. Herpes, by the way, doesn't necessarily have to be a deal breaker. I know lots of happy, healthy couples who have been together for years, and one of them has it, the other one doesn't. It is manageable. But it can be so easily spread that it's one more good reason not to sleep with anyone until you've had a serious talk, both about your health and your monogamous relationship.

I don't think there's a woman out there who hasn't made the mistake of assuming her man is monogamous. "I'm not sleeping with anyone else, and he's not the player type, so I'm sure he's not sleeping with anyone else either," she reasons. Girlfriend, nothing could be further from the truth. Most men sleep around. This doesn't mean they're dogs, it just means they're human. They do it because we allow them to. In fact, until you have the exclusivity talk in the sober light of day, it's safe to make the assumption that he is indeed sleeping with other women, and you're not about to become a member of his harem. Don't make the mistake of thinking that your skill on your back or on your knees will convince him that he wants you and only you. It's your vertical skill that will make him want to commit. A blow job is a blow job is a blow job to men, and just so they're dipping their wickets regularly, they're not going to be picky about who's doing it. When it comes to members of the opposite sex, never assume a damn thing. It all must be clearly spelled out between you.

"But what if I'm horny?" you might ask. "What if he's driving me crazy, and I want to sleep with him so bad my teeth hurt?" I say kiss him good night, then run home to your bedside table and jump on the vibrator. Always make sure you have plenty of batteries on hand. "But what if it's Saturday night and I absolutely hate waking up alone on Sunday mornings?" you might ask. Get yourself a dog or a cat, or make a standing date for Sunday breakfast with your girlfriends. They're far less dangerous and complicated.

On Beyond Sex

There are specific, clear-cut rules for setting physical boundaries during the first ninety days of infatuation. No commitment; no sex. That's all there is to it. Social boundaries, however, are a bit tougher to define. You have to keep your own comfort level in mind while being considerate of his. How often do we see each other? How often do we phone, text, or email? When do we meet each other's family or friends? How high a priority do we expect to be in each other's lives?

The only way to resolve all these issues is through open communication. If something is bothering you and you're having a hard time talking about it in a mature, calm, non-accusatory way, it's not a good sign. It could be that he doesn't make you comfortable expressing your feelings, but it could also mean that you're letting your insecurities rule you, you're being unreasonable, or you're just too much of a hothead. I'm going to give you a couple of examples of good and bad ways to establish comfort in a relationship during the first ninety days.

Maura and David

David was a handsome, successful member of the Millionaire's Club who was not only looking for a wife, but a stepmother to his three young children. Maura was a beautiful, well-educated professional and a single mother as well, and I knew they'd be a good match, so I suggested they go out. David was reluctant to meet her at first, because he didn't like the pictures I showed him. In all honesty, they didn't show her in her best light. This is yet another reason why I encourage everyone to spend some money on professional photos. Remember, to get a better man, you need a better photo. Anyway, I convinced him to ask her out in spite of this, and he decided that a nice dinner couldn't hurt.

Halfway through the dinner they called me on David's cell phone to tell me what an amazing time they were having and to thank me for the terrific match. It's calls like that that make it all worthwhile for me. Weeks went by, and I got several thank-you notes from both David and Maura. They were dating regularly and were enjoying each other immensely. They both agreed that they would introduce each other to their children when the time was right, and they set everything up for the best possible outcome.

After the first thirty days, however, a problem arose. As beautiful and intelligent as Maura is, she can also be a little needy, a little shy, a little emotional. One scary Sunday, I got a very angry call from David, telling me that Maura had done something absolutely unacceptable, and he never wanted to hear from her again. As a dutiful matchmaker, I'm willing to be the bearer of unpleasant messages, but in this case, I knew I better get both sides of the story, and this is what I was able to surmise:

David and Maura went out on a Friday night, and he asked her if she wouldn't mind if he took her home early because he wasn't feeling so great and thought he might be coming down with something. Maura felt a little hurt, but obliged. All day Saturday she waited by the phone for him to call, as was his habit, but no call came. Neither did he email or text. The next day was Sunday, and she still hadn't heard anything from him. She became frantic. She was sure there was something tragically wrong—he was probably seeing someone else! She'd been cheated on before—she knew the drill. She also knew where he lived, so she decided she'd drive over unannounced and catch him in the act. If he wasn't home, she'd wait for him in her car in front of his house. There was no way she would let him get away with this!

She knew she'd made a terrible mistake when she saw David pull into his driveway and get out of his car with his baby daughter in his arms, wrapped in a blanket. The other two children were in their pajamas, with red noses and blurry eyes. It seems that David had contracted a bad case of the flu from his children, and they were all just returning from an urgent-care facility. Imagine his surprise to see an upset Maura, whom he had not yet introduced to his children, sitting in her car in front of his house. The kids couldn't help but notice the strange woman. He controlled his anger and asked her to leave, which she did, fully aware that she'd completely blown it with him.

David is not a very forgiving person, but I was finally able to convince him to cut her a little slack. I stood by my conviction that they were perfect for each other, and told him that I would have a talk with Maura, and she would never act so outrageously again. David eventually did give Maura another chance, and they moved on with the relationship.

Now I must warn you—they had the luxury of a matchmaker to intervene. Chances are that you probably don't. You're going to have to work hard to keep your own insecurities in check, and keep the channels of communication wide open. This is especially difficult in the first ninety days of infatuation, because emotions and passions are on the surface, and you probably haven't settled down into a comfortable, consistent groove yet. Be very careful, and don't act hastily. Take a cue from Cindy.

Cindy and Mark

Cindy was a beautiful, twenty-six-year-old, Midwest-born college grad, living her life to the fullest in LA. She was making great money and appeared to have it all, but she just couldn't seem to meet the right guy. One weekend she and her girlfriends took a road trip to Las Vegas, as Angelenos often do, and there she met a tall, dark, and handsome Boston boy named Mark. He had actually grown up in Santa Monica (a beach community of LA), and his parents still lived there. Cindy and Mark seemed to have everything in common, and they just clicked. While they were physically attracted to each other, they were both intent on building a friendship first, and shared a true sense of camaraderie. It helped that their friends got along well with each other. The two groups merged and became one of the happiest parties in Vegas.

The only fly in the ointment was the fact that they knew they'd have to part on Sunday night. He would fly back to his real estate investment job in Boston, she would go back to Los Angeles, and it would be difficult, at best, to see each other. But there was that one thread of hope, since his parents still lived in California.... They returned to their respective homes and kept in contact by phone, and discovered that they were even more in sync with each other than they'd thought—they'd both planned on going to Miami several weeks later for spring break! (they're under thirty, remember.)

Mark invited her to stay in his hotel room with him and promised to be a perfect gentleman—there would be no hanky-panky whatsoever, if she wasn't comfortable with it. She told him she truly appreciated that, because, in truth, she was a little gun shy. She'd recently extricated herself from a terrible relationship with a passive-aggressive man, and she knew that if she hadn't slept with her ex on the second date without a commitment, she never would have gotten into that mess. Cindy told Mark she would be delighted to stay with him if they could go the friendship route, and he was happy to oblige. He even covered all the expenses, and wouldn't let her contribute a dime. When a work emergency arose in Boston and he had to fly back two days early, he covered her hotel expenses for the remaining two days, even though he wouldn't be spending them with her.

The chemistry and friendship between them couldn't have been stronger, so next he invited her to visit him in Boston. Since they were still just friends, she wouldn't allow him to pay for her plane fare, but he covered all the expenses once she arrived, was the perfect host, and a perfect gentleman. They began to get a little physical, and the chemistry was great! But they both knew exactly where to draw the line, and that was about three steps short of intercourse. Long passionate kisses okay, but no nudity whatsoever.

The more time she spent with him, the more attracted she became, and she found herself desiring to be much closer to him. In the next several weeks she planned to attend a bachelorette party in Las Vegas with her girlfriends, and she invited him to meet her there again. He gladly accepted the invitation but had to cancel at the last minute, again because of business obligations. With the real estate market just beginning to crash, he had urgent negotiations that needed his immediate attention.

Cindy came to me teary-eyed and upset. "I want something more," she told me, "but I don't know how to get it. It's so complicated! I'm the one who drew the line in the first place. So far I've done all the traveling to see him. He hasn't inconvenienced himself at all to come and see me. If he was going to cancel Las Vegas, he should at least offered to come out here and see me another time—I mean, his parents *do* still live here. Why can't he come and see me?"

"Why should he?" I asked. "Dry your tears—we can fix this—it's nothing," I comforted her. The fact of the matter is, since Cindy had set up the "friendship" boundaries, Mark had no reason whatsoever to go out of his way to see her. As much as I'm sure he enjoyed her company, a guy is not going to make an effort to fly clear across the country to see someone he has no hope of ever going deeper with, if you catch my meaning. She needed to start sending a different message.

"Who was the last one to communicate?" I asked. Because they were twenty-somethings, they texted each other more than they called. Since she was the last one to text him, I told her she had to wait until he texted back. She wouldn't have long to wait. He was consistent and usually contacted her around dinnertime, when he'd have the opportunity to give her his undivided attention. As soon as his "What RU doing?"

message popped up on her BlackBerry, she was to ask if it was a good time to talk, and if he said yes, she was to call him and actually talk to him about this. A phone call is so much more personal! It's more immediate, and you can hear the nuances in the other person's voice. Under no circumstances was she to text about her important feelings. I told her to use her sweetest, sexiest voice, and say the following:

"Mark, I want to tell you that it's been really fun meeting you and spending time together. I know that we've had some major chemistry. It's clear that we're very attracted to each other. But I was worried about the distance between us when we first met, and that's why I thought it would be better if we were just friends. But the more time we talk on the phone and the more time we spend together, the stronger I feel the connection. I'm not looking for a text/email/phone buddy, though. In order for me to move on to the next level [notice the use of the term "next level"—less crass and intimidating than saying, "in order for you to ever get a piece of this"], I need to see you in person. Now, I've come and met you twice in Boston and Miami. I was really hoping you could make a trip out to California to see me. After all, your family lives here, and you could visit them at the same time."

Cindy wrote it all down, gave him the speech, and was met with silence for a few long seconds. Then he said, "You know what? You are absolutely right." While they were still on the phone he went online and bought a plane ticket. Two weeks later she was picking him up at LAX. Before she knew it, they were entering the three to six month phase, and were ready for their Relationship Reality Check.

STEP SEVEN

Relationship
Reality Check

Congratulations! You've made it! You two are an official couple now, and the world knows it. No more of that fluttery, one-false-move-and-it's-curtains feeling. But after the first ninety days, reality sets in. On the one hand, you're much more at ease around each other, but on the other hand, every little thing he does isn't quite so cute anymore.

During this period the funky little habits rear their ugly heads. It is no longer practical for you to rush home every time you need to defecate. Yes, your shit does stink, and you're both going to have to get used to it. I have a longtime friend who not only refrains from pooping at her boyfriend's house, she won't poop in a public place whatsoever, and shows open disdain for anyone who does. She is still single—and still constipated—to this day. I believe she always will be.

This is when you get to ask yourself, "Can I live with all his crap?" (literally). I would advise you to go easy on him when it comes to basic body functions. Farting, snoring, burping, chewing his food wrong—these are not character flaws, and certainly should not be deal breakers. Maybe he was raised in a house with mostly brothers, and they think farting and burping is funny. I knew a professional football player who had the most disgusting eating habits—he shoveled everything into his mouth at lightning speed and never took the time to savor, or even taste, his food. Turns out he was raised in a family with eight brothers and sisters, and if you didn't eat fast, there would be nothing left. Then when he was in college, it was the same story at the training table. His girlfriend (who eventually became his wife) got around that by wisely preparing more than enough food at each meal, then asking him how it tasted as he ate, so he would have to slow down and pay attention to what he was eating. And nothing was ever wasted. This was a guy who thought leftovers were a grand treat. These two are happily married today.

Consider this: if he has habits that annoy you, you probably have habits that annoy him too. Yes, girls do snore. Sometimes we sneeze strangely or snort when we laugh. Women love to talk fast, interrupt, and change the subject all over the place. Sometimes we sound like the legal disclaimer at the end of a radio ad, especially if you're from the East Coast like me. What do you do with your gum or your tissues after you're done with them? How do you handle all the issues surrounding your period? Did it ever occur to you that some of your habits might not be so cute after all? During this phase, you learn to live with each other's minor physical annoyances, and you learn to be grateful to each other for doing so.

Move In with Him, Move Out of the Marriage Zone

You might be so caught up in making each other happy that living together seems a natural and normal step. But again, I say unto you, whatever you do, DO NOT MOVE IN WITH HIM! I can't stress it enough. I know I've said this before, but you should never give up your precious freedom and independence until you are absolutely committed to spending the rest of your lives together, and this means you are wearing an engagement ring on your finger, you've picked a wedding date, and your parents have met each other. I have instances of this in my club all the time. Marcus and Shania were a couple that I fixed up. From the moment he laid eyes on her, he knew she was the one and popped the question by the end of the first date. Shania was shocked and flattered and much to her surprise, she was open to the proposal. Marcus, Johnny-on-the-spot, took his Howard University class ring off his finger and put it on hers.

Marcus lived in Atlanta, while Shania lived in Dallas. He was in Dallas for the weekend and, since they were now "engaged" Shania decided to take him to church with her family on Sunday and have him over for supper afterward. He charmed the pants off of her maternal grandmother, complimented her mother, and sat on the porch drinking Courvoisier with her father afterward. The family was sold.

Marcus, a tall, handsome real estate entrepreneur, known as Atlanta's ultimate player, seemed to be becoming a stayer. He asked Shania to move from Dallas into his penthouse pad in Atlanta. Shania called me up on the phone to tell me the exciting news that they had not only hit it off, but that they were engaged. First I congratulated them, but not without a warning. I told her to slow down, qualify her buyer, and to not move in with him until she had the ring and a wedding date set. I also told her that the school ring didn't count. FYI, when a man spends his hard-earned paycheck, he's serious, no matter if he shops at Zales or Tiffany.

Did she listen? Of course not! It's the girls who are first in their class that are last to take my advice. Before she could say, "I prefer platinum," she'd packed her bags and moved from Dallas to Atlanta to live with the guy! Several months later she was crying to me on the phone, the week before Valentine's Day. Six months had passed since she moved in. Marcus was clearly a man who could afford a ring, but instead told her he was buying her a puppy for Valentine's Day. I told her to calm down, take a deep breath, and compose herself. I didn't say "I told you so . . . ," but I reminded her she must become a boundaries girl. We both agreed to give Marcus one week, just enough time to allow Valentine's Day to pass, and see if he bought her that diamond. If not, she was to pack her bags and move back to Dallas. He never did buy her a ring—not even the puppy. Would you believe he bought her luggage instead? He also complained to her that she was moving too fast, when he was the one who proposed on the first date.

The morning after Valentine's Day I got the call. She was

crying and packing her new luggage at the same time. I told her not to worry, that I would fix her up with her knight in shining armor, if she would promise to never move in with a guy again until she had the ring. Sniffling, she agreed. Back in Dallas a week or two later, I went back to my database for her perfect mate. And there was Tyler, a six feet two, divorced restaurant owner. The fact that he was divorced told me he was able to commit, unlike Marcus. Tyler and Shania became monogamous after three months. Six months from the day he met her, he proposed with a ten-carat diamond ring. Six months later they were married. And she didn't move in with him until the day after their wedding.

I'm just saying that if a guy is getting all the benefits of marriage without actually having to legally commit to sharing one half of everything he owns, why would he get married? Many people claim that if it's just a piece of paper, what difference does it make, "We know what's in our hearts." I'll tell you what difference it makes. When you stand up there and take vows in front of your friends and family, or maybe even just in front of a government official, it takes your commitment to a whole new long-term level. Just ask anyone who has ever been married. You're suddenly far more invested in working things out and preparing a life together— it's not so easy just to pack your things and leave. A man who wants to live with you without marrying you is probably not interested in a lifetime commitment. This trial-run concept is ridiculous. Living together is nothing like marriage because you haven't made the ultimate commitment to one another. Either one of you can walk out the door with relative ease.

Why would you want to waste your time and give up your precious apartment under those circumstances? It's okay, though, to do trial runs without giving away all the keys to the candy store. In fact, those long vacations and weekend swaps—"Your place or my place?"—are crucial.

So at the beginning of the three to nine-month phase, make it clear to the man you've chosen that you have no intention of moving in with him until wedding plans are well underway. It will eliminate that six hundred pound gorilla in the room, and you'll both be free to enjoy each other while keeping your own space and boundaries. He'll know from the start that if he wants you to live with him, he'd better be prepared for marriage—he isn't going to get you full time any other way. If he asks you to move in, smile, give him a big hug and a kiss, look him in the eye, and say sweetly, "Oh, honey, I really appreciate the offer, but I'm a little old-fashioned, and I don't want to live with someone until I'm ready to walk down the aisle with him."

An Attitude of Gratitude

You'll both appreciate each other so much more if you look out for each other's best interests instead of focusing only on what you're getting out of the relationship. Whenever I hear some entitled whiner complaining about a great guy I fixed her up with that, "He just doesn't do enough for me!" I always ask her, "So what are you doing for him? And are you expressing enough appreciation for the things he *does* do for you?" Men learn from reinforcement.

An attitude of gratitude is very important during the three to nine month phase. You need to be very grateful for every effort he makes on your behalf, and you need to tell him so. You can throw the 4:1 Rule out the window. You're no longer limited to doing one nice thing for him for every four nice things he does for you. You lose count, because you delight in making each other happy. Because of the degree of comfort and security you feel, you'll both relax into yourselves. You're not so comfortable that you become sloppy and inattentive, but you're beginning to learn how to please each other and are finding out how delightful this can be. He's still on Best Boy behavior, but he's doing it because he wants to, not because he feels he'll lose you if he doesn't. And you feel the same way.

What? You don't feel that way? You're constantly on edge, and you're suspicious that he might be seeing someone else? He's beginning to bore you, and the gardener is looking hotter and hotter every day? Then it's time to bail, my friend. You may have passed the exclusive relationship, First Ninety Days of Infatuation mark, but you're not right together. You might want to make a secret list of pros and cons and see which column is longer. Look at the calendar, and figure out which there are more of: the days you love him, or the days you want to kill him. If you're uncomfortable more than you're comfortable, it's time to throw him back and start fishing for something else. When it comes to relationships, something is not better than nothing. It's better to be single and free than burdened with a bad boyfriend, no matter what your grandchild-crazed mother says. And the sooner you figure this out, the better. None of us are getting any younger here.

Breaking Up Isn't Always Hard to Do

When you've decided that Mr. Right has morphed into Mr. Wrong and that the relationship must come to an end, the last thing you want to do is be cavalier about it. Act like the grown woman you are and tell him you don't want to see him anymore, but do it in the nicest way possible, being very careful not to hurt his feelings or burn any bridges. Aside from the fact that you don't want to deal with an outraged man or a stealthy stalker, it's just part of being a decent human being. And who knows? The next guy you're attracted to could end up being his cousin or colleague. And absolutely refrain, under any circumstances, from a text message breakup. This, of course, is the easiest way out, but it's also the creepiest. Practice the following speech—he'll feel as if an angel gently placed him back down on earth:

"I think you're a great person and a fabulous guy, but it doesn't seem like the chemistry between us is right. [Note you're not making a judgment against him here or blatantly rejecting him.] But I really cherish your friendship, and would love to hang out platonically. Actually, I have a girlfriend who I think you'd probably like much better than me. I'll introduce you to her if you like." Hopefully, he'll give you a referral back and spread word of what a great catch you are through the singles' community.

That's about the nicest way you can break up with someone, and it usually works like a charm. When a man hears that bit about there being no chemistry, he knows that means he's not going to get any more sex, and he'll be emotionally out the door. Many women are passive and feel the need to avoid confrontation, so they lie and say something like, "I'm going to be really busy at work for the next couple of months, so I won't have time to see you." Or, "My ex-boyfriend has come back into my life, and we're going to see how things go." A true hunter male will not let excuses like that deter him; he'll just assume that now is a bad time for you and will keep pursuing you, which will really annoy you.

Honesty is always the best policy, especially if you can easily be spotted on the internet dating sites again or out and about with your friends when you said you would be hunkered down in the office.

When you break up with a man, you'll probably feel quite uncomfortable, if not just plain bitchy. As women we're taught to please people and to never let anyone down. After it's done, however, I promise you'll feel empowered—you didn't let anyone manipulate you, and you stood up for what you wanted, or didn't want, as the case may be. Plus you stopped wasting your precious time with the wrong guy. You've also proven to yourself that you have faith that there's someone else out there for you who is a better fit for you, and you don't need to desperately cling to whatever is right there in front of you. Congratulations! This is a real breakthrough.

Now, what happens if the shoe is on the other foot and, perish the thought, he breaks up with you? My advice to you is to believe him when he says it's over and excise him from your life. Make a clean break. When a man gets up the courage to end things, he's probably been thinking about it for a long time. He's either so miserable in the relationship that even regular, easy sex isn't worth sticking around for, or, and this is most often the case, he's found someone else who is all too eager to provide that regular, easy sex for him.

Don't be naïve and buy into that crazy rationale your friends will tell you to comfort and console you: "He'll be back, I know he will—you're the best thing that ever happened to him." By the way, NEVER tell a man, "I'm the best thing that ever happened to you." If he believed that, he wouldn't be breaking up with you, and you're not exactly in a great position to convince him.

Also, don't go for the lame theory that "He'll get tired of her and come crawling back to me," or "Wait until he sees what it's like out there—he will return." I've heard relationship specialists claim that nothing is really over until ninety days after he says good-bye, so don't lose hope until he's been gone a good three months. Ladies, that's bullshit and only encourages you to stalk him. The one theory you should live by is that once he says *adios*, he is gone, baby, gone. Cut all ties and move on. If he does want to come back, it's because the other girl didn't work out, and you're sloppy seconds.

To truly cut ties you must get rid of, or hide, all pictures you have of him, all the gifts he gave you, delete anything that reminds you of him from your life, including his phone numbers and his email address. Avoid the places you know he'll be. NEVER cruise his house. Above all, and this is consummately important, NO BREAKUP SEX! You might think you can handle it, "just this one last time," but I'm telling you right now, you can't. As soon as you start rubbing up against each other, the oxytocin kicks in and you start thinking, "This will remind him how great we are together and he'll stay. Surely he won't want to leave this behind." Just because he wants to sleep with you after you've broken up does not mean he's entertaining thoughts of getting back together. He is merely entertaining thoughts of an easy lay. The sooner you get that through your head, the cleaner the breakup will be, and the less inclined you'll be to come across as a pathetic stalker.

Bye-Bye Net

So if you make it to the three to nine month point without a nasty breakup and it seems that all systems are go, it's time for both of you to cut off all your other options. Stop attending singles' activities, going places where you used to meet single men, and, most important of all, take all your dating profiles off the internet singles' sites and freeze your membership with the matchmaking service you might have joined. You should tell him you're doing this, and he should do the same, if he hasn't already. In order to give this relationship the attention and dedication it deserves, you both need to commit completely and not even stick one pinky toe in the dating pool. This is the only way for you both to honestly roll up your sleeves and work on the relationship at hand. No excuses for leaving your profiles up are acceptable.

I frequently hear ridiculous reasons like, "It was too complicated to take my profile down," or "I paid for a full six months and I can't get out before then." Believe it or not, those excuses are usually made by women, not men. Men pride themselves in being internet savvy enough to master their online activities. My male members of the Millionaire's Club complain about this all the time. They call me, whining, "She claimed to be seeing only me, and was I ever embarrassed when my best friend found her profile online and began hitting on her!" I've had more breakups over this than I can count, and I don't blame them for being upset. Ladies, now is the time to shut out all other distractions. A Pair and a Spare no longer applies at this point. Keep your best friend handy, but get rid of the backup guy. If your man has gotten to the point where he's willing to commit to you, you need to commit to him.

Money Talks

More important than the amount of money he makes is his attitude about money and how to spend it. During this important six-month phase, you are going to find out if he believes money is the root of all evil, or that money makes the world go 'round. You need to find out if you agree with, and/or can live with his attitudes. Think about it: if you're upset about your finances, the last thing you want to do is have sex, so your love life goes out the window too. It's wise to get money issues out of the way up front, so there are fewer surprises or arguments down the road.

It's important that you two have compatible beliefs about

this all-important subject. Are you savers or spenders? Do you believe it's more important to save for retirement, or to eat, drink, and be merry for tomorrow we die? Do you have good credit? Do you have much debt? You must reveal this to him over this time frame, and he must reveal the same information. Don't sneak around by going through his drawers, file cabinets, or email in-box when he's not home. You should be comfortable enough to be able to ask him directly and you should be ready to reveal the same things about yourself.

Samantha, a good friend of mine, had known her fiancé, Shane, for more than two years yet they'd never discussed his actual financial position. They knew where they were going in the future—they planned to buy a house together, and he would move into her condo so they could save more quickly for a down payment. They were planning on splitting all housing expenses right down the middle. Samantha was a property owner and knew her credit was spotless, and she made the mistake of assuming that Shane's was too. Two weeks before the wedding, Shane started having his mail forwarded to Samantha's address—they were old-fashioned and didn't want to move in together until they were officially husband and wife. Credit card statements and important looking legal documents started filling Samantha's mailbox, and while she respected Shane's privacy, she listened to the nagging little voice inside her, which she later realized was her all-important feminine intuition. It was saying, "Open his mail! Open his mail!" First she opened what looked like a Visa statement. He had a $19,000 balance! She didn't even need to look at his other credit card bills. She did open a few of the envelopes with attorney's addresses, however. She discovered he'd declared bankruptcy three years ago, and was still paying off creditors and legal fees. Samantha was livid! If he had kept this from her, what else was he hiding? First she called Shane, then she called off the wedding. She spent what would have been her honeymoon in Cancún with an old college roommate in Banff.

You need to know the financial basics about your man and, incidentally, you need to be completely honest and provide him with the same information. In order to be truly ready for marriage, you need to have a handle on your own finances. There are plenty of women out there who believe some rich, handsome prince is going to come along and rescue them from their dragons of debt, but I have news for them: princes only exist in fairy tales. Your stock on the dating market goes way down if you're in financial trouble, or if you have giant credit card balances. If you can't handle your own finances, why should a man trust you with his? To be completely and brutally honest, you don't deserve to be rescued. You need to figure it out for yourself and not expect someone else to bail you out. Princesses also only exist in fairy tales.

He Either Provides or Subsides

The bottom line is that most women want a partner with a sense of providership. I'll bet even the Great Oprah, who can easily provide herself (and the entire population of Chicago) with anything her heart desires, wants a man who can pro-vide her with something she needs. It's instinctual with us women. Back in our cave-dwelling days, we needed men who could provide food and protection for us while we laid low, bearing children. Those days may be long gone, but we still like to feel protected. As long as there are people who take advantage of us because we are women, we will appreciate someone stepping in to even the playing field.

On the flip side, most men want to be the major bread-winner and give their wives the choice of staying home and raising the babies while they go off to slay the dragons at work. Unfortunately, we live in a time where the economy doesn't always allow us that luxury. It's not like it's the '50s anymore. It's all about the fact that they'd like to if they could. It's the thought that counts.

During the three-to-nine-month period, you'll find out if he's willing to provide for you or expects to be provided for. When you're browsing through the real estate section on a lazy Sunday morning and you point out your dream house, does he break out in a cold sweat, slam his coffee cup down on the table, and yell, "Geez, you're high maintenance! I could never afford something like that!" Or does he say, "It would be great to be able to afford that house some day. Let's figure out a way to do it!" This is the period when men who aren't marriage-minded men revolt. You'll hear them whin-ing, "How come I have to pay for everything?" and, "You make more money than I do, you should have to pay most of the time!" You'll especially hear this from men who were spoiled as children and had mommy and daddy pay the way.

Because you're a woman, and as such you were raised to be a pleaser, your first response will be, "I guess he's right—maybe I should pick up the check more often." Don't fall into this trap, unless you're comfortable being the masculine one in the relationship. Some women are—they're well suited to the feminine men. But if you prefer to be the one in the relationship with the predominance of feminine energy, you will take his whining about money to be a sign that he is not intent on providership and adjust your circumstances accordingly.

The man who feels a strong sense of providership might not make a lot of money, but he'll come up with ways to spoil and pamper you in spite of this. Free concerts and picnics in the park, matinees and ice cream, going over to friends' houses for dinner, or romantic, candlelit dinners or barbecues at home. This marriage-minded man is resourceful, and he'll do everything he can to make a happy life instead of expecting someone else to bring it to him on a silver platter.

During the three to nine month relationship reality check, you'll also need to discuss lifestyle choices in depth. Do you believe in marriage? Do you want children? If so, how many? If you got pregnant and decided you wanted to stay home with your children, could he, would he afford that? Would he insist on your being at home, even when you're ready to go back to work? If so, could you afford a nanny (preferably an ugly one)? If you got a huge promotion that required relocation, would he be willing to move for you? Would you be willing to move for him? Is he content to live in a rental, or does he intend to buy a house with you? If so, how would you divide the down payment and the monthly mortgage payments?

My friends Libby and Jonathan worked this all out perfectly during their relationship reality check period. Jonathan hadn't proposed yet, but they knew they loved each other enough to get married, and they wanted to get to know each other better, so they were taking their time. Libby owned her own condo, and Jonathan had been living in a large, rent-controlled house for ten years. One day over brunch he said, "You know, I'm really ready to buy a house. I've just been waiting for the right person to do it with. What about you? Ideally, where do you see yourself living in the next couple of years?"

Libby was thrilled when she heard this. She'd always wanted to own an actual house with a garden and two cats in the yard. But she knew that on her single income a condo would be about the best she could afford by herself. She told Jonathan that when the time was right, she'd happily sell her condo and use the proceeds for half of a down payment. He told her he had plenty saved for the other half. Discussing it further, they decided that since he was making about twice as much as she was annually, he would chip in for twice as much of the house payment. A year later they were married and living in a beautiful home that neither one of them would have been able to afford without the other. Every time I go over there for a barbecue, Libby thanks me for coaching her on what to look for and helping her recognize and negotiate it once she found it.

Pick Your Battles

It's all about negotiation during this period, and the wise woman knows how to pick her battles. Is that annoying thing he's doing really worth a fight, or can you bring it to his attention in a nonthreatening way? For example, a gorgeous woman whose boobs are practically falling out of her dress walks into the room. Everyone, including you, is staring at her. You:

A. Whack your boyfriend and loudly tell him to put his eyes back in his head.
B. Angrily storm away and give him the silent treatment for the next half hour.
C. Turn away and start aggressively flirting with the most handsome man in the room.
D. Say to your boyfriend in wide-eyed wonder, "Check out that cleavage! I wonder how much those cost her poor, mammary-obsessed ex-boyfriend."

I don't think I need to tell you which answer is correct. Before you get angry with him and start arguing, ask yourself if it's really worth the unpleasantness. You know how you are when you get mad—your face turns red, your eyes grow hard and dark, your voice raises, you say nasty things you really don't mean, and you call him names you didn't even know you understood. Is that the way you want to treat someone you love? Do you want the man you intend to marry to see you in such an unflattering rage? Take a walk if you have to. Count to 753. It's not that you're never allowed to express anger. It's just that you should do it when you're in complete control and perfectly capable of negotiating the situation to your complete advantage.

The old cliché, "You catch more flies with honey than vinegar," has not been repeated through the ages for nothing. When you're angry with him, it's usually because you want him to change his behavior. You'll get a lot further with him if you discuss it rationally than if you viciously lash out. The good negotiator always begins by assessing if it's a good time to talk. She then continues with a compliment and moves on to the negotiations from there.

For example, your boyfriend promises he'll come by to see you after his best friend's bachelor party, even if it's late. You don't hear from him until the next day. You're pretty sure he didn't call you because he was drunk, and/or did some things he's too ashamed to admit. When he finally calls, you are seething. You can either yell and cry and scream and threaten to leave him, or you can calmly say, "This is not the best time for me to talk. I was really looking forward to seeing you last night—you're so sexy after you've been out with the boys. But when you didn't even call, I was worried, disappointed, and angry. I'm still dealing with that, so I'd rather not talk to you right now. I'll call you back when I've cooled down." I can almost guarantee that he'll be at your door in twenty minutes, bearing flowers and his most ingratiating smile. By withdrawing from him, you're actually pulling him closer.

John Gray is 100 percent correct when he says, in *Men*

Are from Mars, Women Are from Venus, that men are like rubber bands, and if you let them go far enough, they'll eventually snap back. He also wisely and accurately states that men need to go into their caves sometimes, and you should leave them alone in there so that they can think and brood and reevaluate, and they'll love you more for allowing them that.

Men also need time to run around and do manly things with their buddies. The smart woman doesn't begrudge her man his friends; rather, she encourages them to go off together—she prepares food for their poker nights, then excuses herself to go see a movie with her girlfriends. When she meets his friends, instead of resenting them for taking him away from her, she flatters them, she befriends them. She even flirts with them just a little. You want them to say, "Man, if you guys ever break up, can I have her phone number?" rather than, "Dude, when are you going to get rid of that old ball and chain?"

You Can't Change Him, But You Can Train Him

It's all a matter of letting boys be boys, and trying to condition yourself to love them just as they are. I laugh at the woman who says, "Yes, my current boyfriend has a few rough edges. I can polish them off." Or, "He's great raw material—I can work with him."

Wrong attitude! That implies you want to mold him into something he's not. Would you really respect a man who would allow you to do that? And who in the hell do you think you are that you can dictate how someone else should walk, talk, and act? Who died and made you God? Every man is fine just as he is, but perhaps he's fine for someone else, and not for you. If you can't love and accept him the way he is, you can't love and accept him ever. Period.

BUT—you can train him. Just like you can't change a Rottweiler into a golden retriever doesn't mean you can't train the Rottweiler to act in a more civilized manner and obey the rules of the house. Training a dog is not so very different from training a man. You do it with a maximum of love and encouragement and a minimum of harsh discipline, and you reward them. You can be stern, but never yell or lose your temper. Every time your man does something good, you reward him with a smile, a hug, a kiss, kind words of encouragement, or anything else that shows appreciation. It might take him a few tries to get things exactly right, but with a little encouragement from you, he'll figure it out.

This is how I trained my ex to take me to the theater and get the exact seats I want. When *Wicked* came to Los Angeles, every time we'd pass a sign for it, I'd say, "Oh, I'm so eager to see that! It looks fantastic! I bet you'd really like it too. Lisa's husband loved it, and you guys sort of have the same taste." When the ads would come on TV, I'd kiss him on the cheek and whisper in his ear, "Wicked." Then I'd change it up a little: "Sheila took her mother to see *Wicked* for Mother's Day, and they got fabulous seats, fourth row orchestra, from some guy on eBay. She said they weren't even that expensive." Notice I told him what I wanted to see and where I wanted to sit, and without whining about it. When he popped up with the tickets, I lavished him with praise, and a lot more than that after the show. He's now first in line to get tickets to all the new musicals that come to town—and he's straight!

Is He Trying to Change You?

Just as you shouldn't try to change him, you should be aware of whether or not he's trying to change you. Is he always making suggestions about what you wear, eat, say, or do, or does he accept you for who you are? If you feel inferior around him, it's probably because he's constantly harping on you to change or picking at you for this or that. Be careful if you catch him asking you, "Are you going to eat that?" "Are you going to wear that?" "Could you please try to remember not to . . . ?" "You really could use some . . ." etc.

It's a different story if he's trying to help you, as my friend Tiffany's boyfriend did. One day at breakfast he said to her, "One of the things I love about you is that you're an educated, well-spoken woman with a lot of valuable information to share. I think people would receive you better if you didn't say, 'you know?' quite so much. You probably don't even realize you're doing it, but sometimes you say, 'you know?' twice in one sentence. Try paying a little attention to it in other people's speech, and you'll see what I mean. Most people use it far too often." Tiffany was not even aware she had been saying "you know?" at all. But when she started listening for it in other people's speech, she realized how foolish it made them sound. It took her a while, but she rid herself of the nasty habit, and she was grateful to her boyfriend (who is now her husband) for pointing it out. He wasn't trying to change her, he was trying to elevate her, and he did it in a very sensitive way, without belittling her. She's used his own trick on him since then—especially in training him to stop ending his sentences with prepositions. Okay, so they're both grammar freaks. That's one of the reasons they're so good together.

The L-Word

When you're in the three to nine month period, three of the most beautiful words in the English language should come up: I love you. He might have used them before this point, but if he doesn't tell you this within nine months of your first date, he is emotionally and/or verbally constipated and you might want to rethink your relationship. The reverse of this can also drive you nuts, however. Some touchy-feely types say, "I love you" to everyone and their dog. "Thanks parking attendant—I love you, man." "Hey there, puppy! I love you!" Then he looks at you with puppy dog eyes and says, "I just love and appreciate you so much!" on the second date. How do you know what the word "love" means to this guy? Until he is looking straight at you and says those three words straight, with no qualifiers, all bets are off. Now, if your man hasn't said it yet, or at least hasn't said it in a significant way, this is the one area where I actually encourage the woman to take the lead and use the L-word first.

"What?" you cry. "Patti Stanger is actually advocating that

the woman take the lead for once?" Well, yes, although ideally he says it to you first and you respond in kind, if you're
feeling it. But it can actually be an effective test of where he
is emotionally. If you're going to tell him you love him first,
make sure you use those three potent words as a reward for
something wonderful he's done, and make sure it's a big thing,
not like buying you one long-stemmed rose: after he's given
you a beautiful gift, taken you away on a lavish vacation, put
your mother up in a nice hotel while she was visiting, or given
up floor-seat Lakers tickets to the NBA playoffs simply because you got the stomach flu. He has to have gone way above
and beyond the call of duty, perhaps financially, but more
important, emotionally. Then you can look him in the eye
and say in all sincerity, "Thank you so much! I love you."

Then see what he says. If he reciprocates, you know you're
on the right track. If he drops his gaze and hems and haws a
little bit, changes the subject, or even murmurs a weak, "Me
too," you could have a problem—you know your feelings are
stronger for him than his are for you, that he's just not very
good about verbally expressing his emotions, or, worst case
scenario, he simply doesn't feel it. Don't push him or scold
him, and above all, never ask a man, "Do you love me?" Just
how exactly is he supposed to answer that? If he does love
you, he has probably been waiting for just the right time and
place to tell you so, and you've gone and ruined it for him. If
he doesn't love you, he knows he's in a heap of trouble, and
so you're leaving him no alternative but to lie. If he doesn't
mirror your sentiments of love when you express them, you
can adjust your attitude accordingly. But if he says, "I love

you" right back, joy of joys, it's time to do an internal happy dance. You two are on the same page, and you could be headed down the same path—to the altar.

Here are some other, beautiful little signs that you're headed in the right direction together:

- He's planning your dates. He makes an effort to see that they're special and adores surprising you by saying things like, "Dress up tonight, I'm taking you someplace you'll love, but it's going to be a secret until we get there." One bit of advice: ask him if you need to take a wrap. My friend Torrie dressed up in a strappy cocktail dress when her boyfriend told her he was taking her someplace "really special," and it turned out he'd gotten box seats at a professional hockey match. With the wonderful buffet and drinks and interesting people, it was indeed special, but Torrie was so cold she couldn't enjoy it.
- He constantly tells you how beautiful you are, even when you're bloated with PMS and wearing sweats, unwashed hair, and glasses.
- He's proud of you and introduces you as his girlfriend to his family and friends.
- He constantly talks about the future and makes plans with you months in advance. For example, in August he asks, "How much time can you take off at Thanksgiving? I'd really like to spend it in Cancún. Can your family spare you for Thanksgiving if we promise to spend Christmas with them?" (BTW, this is such a great sign

that you should prepare yourself for a ring and a proposal on Christmas or New Year's Eve.)

- He starts using the term "we" more than "I." Don't you just love it when he first uses that word, as in, "We need to go to the grocery store," rather than "I need to go to the grocery store"? Your heart skips a beat, and you think, "You mean we're a we? Wooo Hoooo!"

- He clears a drawer for you or cleans out space in his closet, and he asks for the same at your place.

- You find yourself driving together through chic neighborhoods on Sunday afternoons; you might even stop in at an open house or two. You talk about your dream house—the one you'll live in together some day.

- You talk about your favorite names for children, or, if you're past that stage, you talk about the breed of dog, cat, or other pet you'd like to have together.

- He offers to fix things around your house. He shows up at your door with a toolbox and a little bag from Home Depot, to fix things around your house like a washer in your sink or a running toilet, without you asking him.

- He stocks his kitchen with your favorite food and drink. Does he buy guacamole for you, even though he hates avocados? Or maybe he comes home with a six-pack of Diet Coke even though he can't stand the stuff.

- He offers to take care of car repairs and maintenance for you. He may not do it himself, but if you're like me, just having someone else take the car in and deal with the service people is a godsend.

- He asks your advice about work projects or situations. This is especially flattering if you know very little about his profession. It shows he values your judgment and wants to do things that you admire.
- He offers to get you a deal on the tedious, burdensome things you hate dealing with. Most of us love to shop for clothes, furniture, etc., but when it comes to insurance, home repairs, and even taxes, we would ideally have someone we trust take care of all that for us. Mr. Right will.
- He buys things for you—whether he takes you on a shopping spree and treats you to several outfits or picks out simple earrings for you from a street vendor, he's providing for you. And he never goes on a business trip without bringing something nice back for you.
- He cooks for you. Even if he just throws a couple of burgers on the grill, once again, he's providing sustenance for you. It's very sweet. If he romances you with breakfast in bed, you know he's hooked.
- He takes you to the airport, parks the car in the structure, and takes you as far as security will allow. Then he's waiting for you inside at baggage claim when you return. (By the way, once you get married, that treatment stops.)
- You start doing the grocery shopping together. You make a list of the things you'll need Tuesday night, for example, when you're watching your favorite TV show at his house. One of my clients, a widower, says that grocery shopping with his wife was one of his favorite

things to do. He says he feels like a loser when he's shopping alone and looks forward to the day he can go shopping with his wife again. I tell the girls I introduce to him that they'll know he's serious when he takes them grocery shopping.

- He knows your allergies and tastes and tries to accommodate them. For example, if you're allergic to MSG, he asks the waiter if the food contains it before either of you orders. Or if you hate raisins, he asks if they're in the cookies before he buys them.

- He always makes sure you get home safely. Since you're not living together, there will be times you'll go your separate ways at the end of a date. He will insist that you call him when you get home, if he doesn't follow you in his car and see that you get in the door without a problem. That is the ultimate in thoughtfulness, consideration, and providership. Your man is protecting you. Let him do it.

- He sucks up to your friends. He's no dummy—he knows they influence you, so he attempts to ingratiate himself to them, without being too flirtatious.

- When you have a disastrous day at work and you're at the point of hysteria, he'll leave work to come help you.

- He looks out for your family. Perhaps he drives you home for Mother's Day or brings your dad his favorite wine. One of my clients actually helped his fiancée's mother, who was recently divorced, learn how to date online.

- He takes care of you when you're sick. This includes going out and getting you anything you need at any hour of the day or night, from chicken soup to prescription drugs. If a man holds your hair back while you barf, you know he's a keeper. When you're really sick, he'll take you to the doctor and ask the questions you're too sick to ask.

So, if you can check off the majority of the above signs after nine months of dating, it's time to move on to the next step. This one could well be the most important step of all. You're now ready to Negotiate the Ring, without him realizing you're doing it. Good luck—you're almost there.

STEP EIGHT
Negotiating the Ring

Okay, so you've been with him nine months to a year. It's do-or-die time. You've known each other for three or four seasons, and if you're not sure by now that you could be a lasting couple, you probably never will be. Believe me, you've had enough opportunities to find out what he's really like. If you haven't at least mentioned or discussed marriage at this point, you're wasting your valuable time. I'm not saying that no one ever gets married after they've dated for longer periods of time. It's just that, again, no one's getting any younger here. Why wait to start your lives together, if that's what you're going to do? And if not, why would you want to waste several years or more in a relationship that's never going to have that happy ending you've always wanted?

For those of you who are not interested in marriage, but are comfortable in a relationship without legal bonds, just put yourself on autopilot and cruise. As long as your man is treating you right, you'll have no complaints. Make sure you and your guy are on the same page and want the same things. This way everyone wins.

But if it's marriage you're after, I'm going to give you some strategic advice on how to get it. But first, let's make sure that this relationship is actually going somewhere and that you're not mired in stagnation. We've all been there at one time or the other. I was giving relationship advice on the radio one day, and a woman called wanting to know if she should be concerned because she and her boyfriend have been dating for two and a half years, and he's never used the L-word or mentioned marriage. Concerned? She should have dumped him eighteen months ago! I told her to get the hell out of there—that guy will never be serious with her.

Although it may be evident that he's mentally (not legally) committed by the mere fact that he stuck around that long, it's clear he has no interest in making her happy by marrying her. He put doubt in her mind and this will put her on the defensive and disappoint her. She's in the first of the four stages of romantic enslavement:

1. Doubt
2. Resentment
3. Anger
4. Depression

In the end she loses her power and she has no bargaining chip to negotiate marriage. If you feel any of those emotions about your boyfriend on a regular basis, you've become his romantic slave, not his partner, and it's time for you to start over again. Make a clean break, go directly to Dating Detox, do not pass Go.

We're going for the tough-love strategy here. After nine months to a year, your guy needs to fish or cut bait. But here's the tricky part: you cannot pressure him into it, and you can't give him an ultimatum. Most important of all, *you* cannot propose to *him*. Don't rob him of his shining moment. Men think, plan, rehearse, and dream about their proposals just as much as you do. It's his once in a lifetime chance to stand up and claim his ultimate prize. That is how he looks at it—don't steal the illusion.

As a matter of fact, you can't even allow him to think that the proposal might have been your idea. Remember, he needs to feel like he is the hunter, like he is carefully reeling you in, and not vice versa. This can be a bit of a challenge, but there are some very clever ways to inspire a proposal. This chapter is all about placing him exactly where you want him and making him think it was his idea to go there.

What Are They Afraid Of?

Before you begin to negotiate the ring, you need to know what you're up against. If you've been dating a guy for nine months to a year and he has expressed no interest whatsoever in marriage, it could be because certain doubts and fears are making him dubious about the institution itself. Some of those fears you can put to rest if you play your cards right—and he doesn't even need to know you're on a campaign. But there is only one way to handle other misgivings: you need to politely bow out. I know that sounds tough—maybe even excruciatingly painful. But you'll be doing yourself a huge favor in the long run by releasing him now, instead of twelve years from now, when your butt and boobs are both sagging down to your knees. Ending a relationship with someone who you want to marry is not a pretty picture, but it could happen if you don't pay attention to the following reasons men give for not wanting to get married:

- **Complacency:** He's of the opinion that if it ain't broke, don't fix it. You've made everything so comfortable for him that he's become a relationship couch potato. If he's getting free rent, why would he buy the house, especially when interest rates are so high? You're probably doing everything for him, from his laundry to his grocery shopping. You've made everything so comfy inside that he never feels the need to take you out. His friends might have told him that sex goes out the window as soon as he gets married, so why should he wreck his sex life with a ring and a ceremony? You've heard the joke bachelors tell each other: "Why was the bride smiling as she walked down the aisle? Because she knows she just gave her last blow job!" Who wants to be that guy? He is mentally married to you already. In his mind, you've tied the knot to his satisfaction, so why should he do any more?

  Complacency is not fatal to your relationship. If he seems like he's a little too comfortable and therefore not inclined to make a move, you're going to have to do something to motivate him. Shake the tree. You might want to go away with your girlfriends for the weekend and let him see how lonely he is when you're not there to make him breakfast in the morning. Sign up for a weekly class or start a new hobby independent of him to give him a little space. Stop being so available. Don't answer his calls or text him back immediately. You don't want to ignore him, but you're not going to jump. Give him a little taste of what life would be like without you so he'll be inclined to close the deal and never have to live without your devotion. You'll also want to give him what I call a Me-a-matum. We'll get to that later.

- **Money:** He feels he's not financially ready to buy the ring, the honeymoon, the house, to start raising kids—there are myriad things he thinks he can't afford. He might still be paying off his school loans, or paying alimony and child support, and barely has enough for himself, let alone a wife. This could be an especially big issue for him if you have high expectations and a sense of entitlement—if you're always showing him pictures of huge diamond rings in magazines and making him drive through the most expensive neighborhoods where you swoon over the houses that are for sale, the poor guy will think he'll have to work for another thirty years before he's ready to buy you everything you've said you wanted. You might have heard him mention more than once, "I'll get married as soon as I'm financially ready."

If you sense this is an issue, you need to go out of your way to convince him that you'll be happy with a small ring, an intimate ceremony, and a cozy apartment for the first several years of marriage. You're marrying the person, for God's sake, not an object, a party, or a house. You might tell him something like, "Just because I buy myself Gucci shoes doesn't mean I have to live in Bel Air—that can wait." If he persists in telling you he won't get married until he has enough money, sit him down when a talk is convenient for both of you and ask him, "How much money is enough?" Then try to make a plan together so you can both contribute to that amount. If he's worried about finances and you want to marry him sooner rather than later, convince him that you're willing to bring your fair share to the table financially, that the entire burden is not on his shoulders. And why should it be? If your dad wasn't a king, then you're not a princess, so don't act like one.

But in order for him to feel like the provider male, he should contribute 60 percent to your 40 percent, unless you make more money than he does, then it should be 50/50. If 50/50 is completely out of the question—you're a corporate dynamo and he's a starving artist—you may have to go 70/30, but under no circumstances can you let him off the financial hook completely. Think Anne Heche and Coley Laffoon, Jennifer Lopez and Ojani Noa, Britney and K-Fed, or Elizabeth Taylor and Larry Fortensky—all were classic disasters.

- **Family Disapproval:** If his family disapproves of you or your family disapproves of him and he can feel it, this is not so easy to remedy. It may be because yours is an interracial relationship, or just intercultural. It might be because of differing religions or economic levels. Your boyfriend might be holding back on a marriage proposal because he knows his parents would never approve of the match and he doesn't want to disappoint them. It's a bad sign if he hasn't introduced you to his parents yet at the nine months to one year point. If, for whatever reason, one of you is unacceptable to the other's family, you need to assess how important your families are to you. Since you're not going to change them and they're not going to change you, this might be a sticking point that will force the two of you to move on in different, more compatible directions.

- **Perfectionism:** Be extremely careful with this guy. You'll recognize him by his constant efforts to fix you. He may be waiting for you to turn into his idea of the perfect wife, or he may be waiting to find a more perfect model, whichever comes first. He might be putting off permanent plans until you lose weight, finish school, get a promotion, etc. But just when you do, he'll come up with some other reason to delay marriage. Best to put him off—for good. He'll either make you feel like you'll never live up to his expectations, or he'll drop you like a hot coal one day out of the blue because he's met someone else he thinks is better. If you feel like you're involved with a man who is waiting for you to change before he gets serious, don't wait to seriously show him the door.

- **Living in the Dark Past:** He's been married before and it was such a bad experience he's afraid to try again. He might have had a horrific divorce in which he lost a lot of money, suffered public humiliation, and lost custody of his children and had them turned against him. If his parents had a bad marriage as well, that's a double jinx. He could be under the impression that all women are like his mother, or like his ex-wife, and he's lost faith in the institution. He might enjoy living with you, but he's got it in his head that marriage changes women into raging shrews, and he never wants to go through that again.

  You can get around this by distancing yourself as far as possible from the people who have scarred him. When you see someone behaving in ways he has complained about, say something like, "Wow, I don't see how people can act that way. I would never dream of doing something like that." Also, look around you for examples of great, happy marriages and draw his attention to them. Then point out what you think is good about those marriages—why you think they work. My friend Shondra's boyfriend, Kevin, had suffered a bitter divorce several years before they met and seemed to be against marriage altogether. But one night they went out to dinner with Shondra's sister and brother-in-law. They seemed so happy and in love that Shondra couldn't help but ask them, "What's your secret?" The husband then went into a loving explanation of why their marriage worked so well. The whole table was practically in tears before they were through. Kevin was silent, but you could tell he was paying rapt attention. He proposed to Shondra three days later. I kid you not, that was all he needed to hear.

- **Living in the Tragic Past:** He may have had a great marriage to his true love, but death separated them too soon. He's a widower and might feel that if he marries you, he would be betraying her. I have a client like that. Although his wife died of breast cancer five years ago and he felt like he was ready to join the Millionaire's Club, when he gets right down to it, he says he's just not ready to get married again. There is hope for him, however. He's a very sensitive man, capable of profound love, and he's definitely worth the effort. This will take the work of a psychiatric professional, however. He'll need to get therapy. He has too much sadness and anxiety to try to heal on his own and he will be very grateful to you for your patience.

- **Peter Pan:** Peter Pans come in many shapes and sizes so don't be deceived—no matter what he looks like, he'll never grow up. He's a commitmentphobe, because committing to something, anything, would force him to take on adult responsibility and face true intimacy. This is the guy who's over forty, never been married, probably lives in a seedy rental with boxes he still hasn't unpacked, even though he moved in five years ago. Or maybe he's a man about town, very social, and doesn't normally have relationships that last more than three weeks. He usually dates women who are much younger or otherwise inappropriate for him. He says things like, "I don't believe in marriage," or "I've never really been in love." He can't be burdened by a pet, or even a plant. Excuse me, but you should have weeded this one out back at the three-month point. He's never said or done one thing that would indicate he's ready to settle down.

There is no fixing this one. Your only solution is to run—get out before he infects you with some narcissistic, nasty disease. You politely tell him, "Thanks so much! I had a really great time. Now I'm off to find my husband. Buh-by." Under those circumstances, there is the slim, I mean Mary-Kate-Olsen-on-a-diet slim, chance that he might realize what he's lost and grow up overnight. But don't count on it. Be ready to walk, and don't look back. Unless he comes running after you with a three-carat diamond. There are those happy exceptions, like Warren Beatty, but it took a strong woman like Annette Bening to straighten him out.

Ultimate Negotiation: The Me-a-matum

So you've finally decided he's the one—that you want to get married and spend the rest of your life with him. You're confident that he feels the same way about you. You've made your checklist and discovered that he embodies all your Must-Haves and your Non-Negotiables. You are financially, emotionally, physically, and spiritually compatible, and you feel safe with him. He makes you feel loved and cherished. You are calm, not on edge with him, and you trust each other completely. It's time to negotiate the ring, my friend, but it's summarily important for him not to know you're doing it. It's not nearly as difficult as it sounds. Follow these three simple steps, and I promise you, if he's the one, you'll have a proposal within the next three months. If he's not the one, you'll have a new boyfriend within the next three months. Either way, you win!

1. Make sure it's a good time to talk. It should be a time when you're both relaxed, and nothing is pressing you. No phone calls, no texting, no emails; this conversation must be had face-to-face. This is not a conversation for when you're driving in the car and on your way to meet someone. Try it on a lazy Sunday afternoon, when work is behind you both and you haven't yet started gearing up for the week ahead. Ask him if this is a good time to talk. Whatever you do, don't say, "We need to talk." Those words strike fear into a man's heart faster than "It's time to schedule that colonoscopy." If he says that for some reason he's not comfortable conversing right then and there, smoothly and cheerfully abort your plan and reschedule. Don't sound bitchy or frightened. Say something like, "Okay, I didn't want to interrupt what you're doing right now. How about later this evening, after dinner?"

But if when you approach him, he immediately responds with "Sure, honey, what's on your mind?" try to stay calm and keep your heart from pounding though your rib cage. This could be the most important conversation of your entire life.

2. Ease your way into the conversation with a compliment. This will put you both at ease, and fill you with that soft, warm glow. Start small. Talk about something he did for you recently that made you happy—put gas in your car, took the garbage out, picked you up at the dentist after your root canal, changed the lightbulb, whatever. If you're on a roll, go bigger. Let him know that he has made you happier than anyone else you've ever met. That you adore, admire, and love him (admiration is really important to men). This will make him feel like your knight in shining armor, and as if no one can love you like he can. He will be very proud of himself and feel wonderful about you and your relationship.

3. Go in for the kill. This is what's known as the Me-a-matum, but he doesn't need to know that. It's your code word for getting what you want. There's a difference between a Me-a-matum and an ultimatum. **An ultimatum is a demand accompanied by a threat. A Me-a-matum is a suggestion accompanied by a gesture.** It's very important to modulate your voice and your emotions. Stay calm, relaxed, warm, and loving. Smile. Make sure your voice is low, not high and shrill. Then adapt the following to your own particular situation: "We've been dating for nine months now—they've probably been the best nine months of my life, and I've really grown to love you. But I have to be honest with you. When we first met, we both agreed that we were looking for someone to marry. Now that we've come to know and love each other, I'm just wondering if you still think marriage could be in the cards for us. We haven't really talked about it lately. I would never give you an ultimatum, but I'm not the kind of girl who dates someone indefinitely. So if you don't see marriage in our future, then I don't want to hold you up, and I need to be free to find someone else who's on the same page as I am."

NOTE: Most men who are in a comfortable zone do not want to ruin their mojo by going out and having to look for new women to date. That's a lot of work to a guy who has such a sweet setup.

Breathe in, exhale, and get ready. You're halfway there. There are three ways he can respond to your Me-a-matum, and I'll tell you what to do in each instance.

1. "Of course I see a future for us. I wouldn't be here if I didn't. I don't want you to date other people. Just have a little patience—I need to do things in my own time, in my own way." If he says this, congratulations! Hug him, kiss him, and tell him how happy he makes you and that you trust him to do what he thinks is best. But, while holding his hand and smiling into his eyes, you need to tell him this: "I trust you completely, however, I cannot be with you more than ninety more days without some sort of movement toward the future. If I do, I'll start resenting you, because you didn't honor your commitment to me, which won't work well for either one of us."

2. "I'm not quite sure yet. I need a little more time." Hold firm. The missiles have not been fired yet. Calmly ask him

how much more time he thinks he'll need. If he gives you a reasonable answer and says within the next ninety days, smile and tell him, "Great! We can resume the conversation then." But if he tells you "I need a couple of years or more," or, "I'm not ready for marriage right now," or, "I don't know," then you have the option of using the Takeaway Technique as a last-ditch effort to turn things around in your favor.

Salespeople use it all the time. For example, if a salesman is selling a car to a consumer who is indecisive about buying, the salesman might say something like, "I'm not sure a Mercedes is really right for you. How about I call my friend over at BMW?" or, "I'm not sure I'm the right salesperson for you. How about I get you another one?" or, "I know you're really interested in the car, however, I have another person who is also interested in it, and if you're not, that's okay. But I have to know by the end of the day."

The relationship equivalent is to say, "I'm not sure I'm the right girl for you. I would understand if you want to date others." Or, "I'm not sure we're a match, because I'm looking for a marriage-minded man, and you don't seem to have any interest in that." You're not freaking out, demanding, or scolding. Instead, you're holding firm to your desires and letting him know that if he's not the guy, you're ready to bolt. He is going to see you as a woman who knows her own self-worth, which is very attractive to the opposite sex. In business, the advantage goes to the person who's least invested. Act like you're not invested, and you could get the ring.

If he still doesn't budge, you must leave the premises in a timely fashion. He knew whether or not he wanted to sleep with you within the first two minutes of meeting you. Most people know within the first nine months of dating whether or not they could ever marry each other. This is when you'll be glad you didn't move in with him. If you did move in with him, shame on you. You need to start considering finding a place of your own, and letting him know that you're doing it.

3. "I'm glad you brought this up. I've had a great time too, but I don't see this relationship going any further. I don't think marriage is in our future." Ouch! This is the one you hoped you wouldn't get. But believe him when he tells you this. Do not naïvely say to yourself, "He just needs more time." He's actually doing you a favor by telling you the truth now rather than later. Don't argue with him, try to change his mind, tell him all you've done with him, or try to get pregnant. None of these things will work. Don't think of it as the end of your hopes and dreams. Think of it as the glorious freedom to explore new hopes and dreams—with someone else, who is infinitely better suited to you.

You need to thank him and move on, immediately. Don't waste a single minute of your precious time waiting for him to come back. Delete him from your phone, your email, your life. Get up and get out of there, or ask him to. A clean break is so much easier and healthier than a long, drawn-out goodbye, and it will keep you from the delusions that inevitably fill your head during breakup sex. If you've broken my rules by living with him, immediately go to the home of a friend or family member. Vent to someone else; never vent to him. Go to a marriage/family counselor, and if you can't afford one, do a web search for a free clinic. Temples have them, churches have them, cities have them. Go do the crying somewhere else. Whatever you do, do not get into bed with him, fall into the spoon position, and expect it to be a brighter day in the morning. Place all the belongings he left at your place in a box and mail it to him or have someone else drop it off. Have that person pick up your belongings from him. It takes ultimate courage and commitment to end a relationship this way, but you need to be a woman of conviction. This is the most important thing you can do for yourself at this point. Hopefully you love yourself enough to go through with it without looking back.

The Exception: There is an exception to the previously mentioned ring negotiations. If you two live a long distance away from each other, your relationship will progress at a much slower, or a much faster rate. Say one of you lives in New York and the other lives in Philly. When you give him the Me-a-matum, he may say he's not sure and that he needs a trial run. He could say he needs to live with you before he'll know for certain. Ladies, you need to hold your ground here. Do not move in with him until you have a ring and a date. Do not offer to change your entire life for a very uncertain bet. He might be willing to move to your city to try things out, but don't let him move in with you. Make him find his own way and his own place.

But one of the advantages to long-distance dating is that the relationship can come to a head much sooner. The hassle and inconvenience, not to mention the miserable time spent longing for or missing your loved one, can spark a decision much faster. "We know we're in love, why should we continue to deal with these obstacles when we can get married and be together full time?" If you're sure he's the one you want, I say brush your hair, grab your coat, and run, don't walk with him, to the jewelry store.

Warning: Never, I repeat, NEVER have this talk with someone you've never met in person but only communicated with over the internet. That is just plain insane. I've come across people who have left their husbands and wives to travel across the world to meet their online lover face-to-face, only to find out that there is no chemistry whatsoever.

So, if your relationship ends at the Me-a-matum, go back to Step One, Dating Detox. Pamper yourself and prepare yourself to go out and find The One, using all the things you learned from the relationship you just ended. Consider this guy to be training wheels, and be grateful to him and the universe for the invaluable experience. You never would have gotten this far if he didn't have some redeeming features.

The Prenup Is Your Friend

Ladies, if he does take you happily by the hand and starts leading you toward the altar, it's time to start checking into prenuptial agreements. Prenups get a bad rap. Don't be afraid of them; they're actually for your own good, especially if you're older and have had time to accumulate property, investments, or your own business.

If you're a couple of penniless students or recent divorcées who have left everything behind or never acquired anything, prenups may not be so important, but a contract is. Go to an online legal site or one of those storefront legal document places with a notary public and see what you can find. There are all sorts of contracts that could work for you. You probably have more valuable possessions than you think—for example, if you have your grandmother's armoire, and he's just purchased a flat screen TV, if (God forbid) you should split up, you'll want to keep your armoire, and he'll want to keep his flat screen. You can legally designate that.

But what exactly is a prenuptial agreement? They sound so scary and unromantic. Basically, it's a legal document that defines both your assets before you go into the marriage, specifies what will be community property during the marriage, and how that will be distributed if the marriage ends. Remember the divorce rate is at an all-time high, and more than 50 percent of all marriages end in divorce.

In the event of death, a prenuptial agreement can and often does supersede the will. So if your poor husband dies before he gets around to changing his will and including you in it, you are still entitled to the community property as defined in the prenup. Take that, you greedy stepkids!

Look at it as the business side of your marriage There are so many advantages to negotiating any business, professionally, calmly, and unemotionally. The prenuptial agreement has nothing to do with love, affection, or feelings—it just has to do with cold hard cash and property. Many people find it distasteful to talk about splitting up before they even get married, but they should try to see it as a declaration of faith:

"This is everything I have, and here's how we'll share it." It's also a great way to convince your wealthy fiancé (if you have one) that you are marrying him for love, and not marrying him for his money. (Well, you are, aren't you?) Many rich men have been burned by greedy women, and the prenup is a good way to put them at ease about that particular issue.

The prenuptial agreement is also a great way to find out the truth about each other's assets before you legally tie the knot. Your man might be telling you he has a huge investment portfolio, but when he declares his assets in the prenup, you could find he actually has none—that he's in debt. It's also a way to force yourself to assess and come clean about your own assets and help you plan for the future together. It puts a spotlight on your financial situation and encourages you to talk about future goals and how you're going to achieve them.

For example, Carla found her prince (so she thought) through the Millionaire's Club. Dan was a strapping, sexy thirty-nine-year-old hedge-fund kid. He was nouveau riche—came from a dirt poor family, didn't go to college, but hit it big on Wall Street and worked his way up fast. He was perfect in the relationship, courting her and buying her a ring at just the right time. He was almost too perfect, she thought, right up until it came to the prenup.

Carla came from old money, and her father insisted on them having a legal agreement. Dan was reluctant but finally gave in. In preparing for the prenup, it came out that Dan was broke and living beyond his means on credit. It almost destroyed the relationship. There were many harsh words and tears, but Carla and Dan truly loved each other, so she and her father finally concluded that she would marry Dan if he would agree to consolidate his debts, live below his means—no limo or jet service, no lavish dinners or trips, no more gambling. And he would be reporting back to Carla's father on a weekly basis. Carla and Dan are now happily married, have two children, are out of debt, and Dan and his father-in-law are successfully in business together.

This is just one more example of how, if either you or your perfect match bring anything of material value into the marriage, it's best to talk about that before you say "I do." Did you ever stop to consider just how much that business you built up is worth? Don't you want to protect it, so that everything you made from it up to the point of marriage remains yours? I personally have to be very careful about this, and I know a lot of women like me. I've had boyfriends who don't want to sign prenups, because if anything should happen to our marriage, they want half of the pie I baked long before I met them. Screw that! What kind of loser does that? Certainly not one I'd ever want to marry.

And by the way, you should not expect to get part of the business he built up before he ever met you. You two should be willing to split the assets you both accumulate in your respective businesses *after* you marry. That's fair, just, and reasonable.

If he's a trust-fund baby, comes from a wealthy family, or works in the family business, his relatives and business associates may insist on a prenuptial agreement. You should accept it with a stoic, professional attitude, and tell him you'll have your lawyer look it over. Then ask where your attorney should send his/her bill.

And by the way, if it's you or your family that has the lion's share of the assets, you'll want to be especially careful. My wealthy friend Virginia has been trying to get out of her marriage for the past four years, because she and her lazy ex can't come to terms about alimony. Sure, they signed a pre-nup, but when it came to drawing up an agreement about alimony, she brushed right over it, thinking, "Why do we even need to include this? I'd never need to ask him for alimony." She couldn't even conceive that he might be the kind of person who would demand alimony from her. As a result, he keeps trying to get more, dragging her back into court every six months or so. He's also the kind of guy who wants a lot of child support even though he only sees the kids once every other weekend. The court denies all his requests every time, so she doesn't know why he even bothers. Still, it's burden-some and keeps her from moving on.

Another way a prenuptial agreement can protect you is that it can legally separate your assets from his, thus protect-ing you from being responsible for the debts he acquired be-fore he married you—particularly to his ex-wife. Did you know that in many states, if you get married and combine your income with your new husband's, his ex-wife can come back and sue him for more alimony or child support, because it's based on a percentage of his household income, which, when combined with yours, has suddenly increased? For ex-ample, Hagatha, the ex-wife, can say, "He was making sixty thousand dollars per year when we split and we based the alimony and child support on a percentage of that, but now that he's married they're making one hundred ten thousand dollars per year, so we deserve more." You could end up paying for his ex-wife's spa treatments. Exes can be vicious.

Prenups can also save you financially if your marriage goes south much sooner than expected. In many states, if you're married for ten years or more, you automatically split everything you both acquired during the marriage straight down the middle, but if you've been married for less than ten years, everything might depend on who can afford the best attorney. This is where the pre-ten-year clauses come in, which can state something like, if your marriage lasts for one year, you get this much alimony and a sort of leaving bonus, five years, this much, etc. *Sex and the City* fans will remember how Charlotte negotiated this fairly, with a large lump sum of cash and an apartment thrown in. Just like she did, don't be afraid to have your attorney stand up for you and make some changes in the prenuptial agreement your fiancé presents to you. He will expect that, and respect you for not just rolling over and signing.

The prenuptial agreements of the rich and famous include the famous (or infamous) infidelity clauses that you hear so much about. There are rumors that one celebrity couple included a clause that states she gets something like $6 million from her husband if he cheats on her. That's enough to make a guy think twice about a silly little fling. It's also been reported that she has to pay him a smaller amount if she cheats on him. It may sound cold and calculated, but there are special rules for people who move in those circles.

Laws about prenuptial agreements differ from state to state and country to country, of course. As of 2007, the United Kingdom, for example, doesn't even enforce prenuptial agreements, while prenups are automatically part of a legal marriage in Germany, France, Italy, and Canada. In these countries, the prenup is called a "matrimonial regime." Throughout the US, state laws differ, but there are five requirements for a prenuptial agreement to be considered legal:

- It must be in writing—an oral agreement is no good.

- Both parties must sign the agreement voluntarily, and not under duress. No big guys named Guido and Luigi can be standing behind you when you sign.

- There must be full and/or fair disclosure at the time of signing—in other words, neither of you can hide any assets or hold anything back. Both of you have to declare every penny you have and every valuable object you own.

- The agreement cannot be unconscionable, which means it has to be fair to both parties, and not heinously weighted to the advantage of one or the other. In other words, it can't say that if you get divorced, he gets $20 million and you get two dollars.

- It must be legally and lawfully signed and executed by both parties (not their attorneys) in front of a notary public. You can't just wave it off and say, "Let the attorneys take care of it."

Note that prenuptial agreements cannot regulate issues regarding third parties. In other words, your children's rights, no matter what age they are, will not be covered by the prenuptial agreement. And you can't legislate rights for your future children either. So no child support or custody issues can be covered by the prenup. You'll need a separate document for that.

Now do you see how the prenup can be your friend? It may sound pessimistic and unromantic at first, but actually you can use it as an invaluable opportunity to get to know your spouse better and for him to learn more about you. If you and your fiancé are both smart, reasonable, rational people, prenuptial agreements can be a win/win for everyone involved. On a grand scale, look at Ivana and Donald Trump, for example. She and the Donald were married for years and had three children together. When their marriage broke up over his affair with Marla Maples, of course there were fireworks, but there was also an ironclad prenup. Ivana ended up with a nice sum, but she also ended up with a supportive friend for life. It was Donald who comforted her graveside when her father died, and Donald who hosted her recent wedding to Rossano Rubicondi at the magnificent Mar-a-Lago estate in Florida. Ivana may have been bitter when the marriage first broke up, but she was smart enough to know better than to bite the hand that fed her. She negotiated a fortune, and more important, the freedom to date the men of her choice and be on great terms with the father of her children.

You're probably exhausted by now from thinking about romance and marriage in legal/business terms, but I promise you that if you do this by the book (my book), it will save you a fortune in heartache and cash. Please remember that women today are making more money than ever, have more responsibility than they did in their mothers' day, and have to be smart about the future. After all, we do outlive our men by seven to ten years.

Really, it's all about negotiation, from first date to perfect mate. Finding and marrying your ideal match is not so unlike finding and landing that perfect job: just about everything is negotiable, from location to salary to benefits to start date. The skills you learn in Negotiating the Ring will help you in many other aspects of your life as well. The only difference is that when you're negotiating with the man you love, he must never know he's come to the bargaining table. The trick is to make him think that it's all his idea to give you exactly what you need, exactly when you need it. You're a smart girl. I'm sure you can handle that.

Conclusion

Now that you know all my secrets, it's time to start focusing on living happily ever after. Even if you haven't met your match yet, go ahead—buy a bridal magazine or two. Start scanning theknot.com. I'll leave you with one last success story:

My friend Paulina had had it with anything even remotely attached to weddings. She had just attended her sixth wedding in six months, and she wasn't even a bridesmaid at any of those weddings—her own sister didn't even ask her to be her maid of honor. And if her grandmother asked her one more time, "When are you getting married?" she knew her head would explode.

One day, while indulging in a carton of Chunky Monkey, she picked up a famous metaphysics book and read all about manifesting the things you want. Since she wanted nothing but a groom at that point in her life, she decided to give it a try. The book said to "Act as if . . ." meaning to act as if something has already happened. She decided to act as if she were engaged and preparing for her wedding. So she put her grandmother's diamond engagement ring on her left ring finger and went down to her local Saks Fifth Avenue bridal department. The salespeople fawned all over her, pulling out beautiful, creamy, flowing dresses for her. She tried them all on: the Vera Wangs, the Badgley Mischkas, the Monique Lhuilliers, the Valentinos. She looked at herself in the mirror as a chic but blushing bride, and was transformed. The salespeople snapped Polaroid photos of her, and just looking at them made her happy. When she went to bed that night, she slept with the Badgley Mischka snapshot over her heart. She couldn't have been happier if she had a doting fiancé and a wedding date to go along with the dress.

Two weeks later to the day, when she was still reveling in her bridal-gown high, she met Carter at a business networking event. He was the most compelling man she'd ever laid eyes on. He strode right up to her, asked her name, and invited her out, right then and there. He claimed her!

Six months later they were engaged. The dreams of the wedding and the Badgley Mischka dress became realities. Paulina and Carter settled down into domestic bliss, with two children, three dogs, and an iguana.

The powers of the mind, body, and spirit, working together, are the most powerful tools any human being can utilize. And guess what? They're all available to you, any time, anywhere. Just because you can't see them doesn't mean they're not there. And just because you might not be able to see your perfect match standing right there in front of you doesn't mean that he's not out there, being guided in your direction this very minute. As a matter of fact, I am absolutely certain that he is on his way.

If you learn anything from this book, I want you to remember that you have the power to attract Mr. Right For You at any moment. Don't listen to the other men who say you're not pretty enough, skinny enough, smart enough, or rich enough, because you ARE! You are perfect for the man of your dreams. The men who find you lacking are just not right for you.

I've taught you how to clear the way for your ideal mate to come into your life, go places where he's likely to find you, flirt and catch his attention, discern if he's a keeper, and I've instructed you on his proper care and feeding once you decide he's worthy of you. Most important, I've given you the means to negotiate the ring. Use these tools wisely, my friend. May the student surpass the teacher . . . even though the teacher is on the journey with you. I wish you . . . I wish us our own happily ever after.

Here's to the next year of finding true everlasting love and happiness!

XOXO
Patti

Acknowledgments

In order for one to succeed it takes a family. This is my family:

To my grandmother Anne, known as Nana to me, who taught me there is a lid for every pot.

To my mother, Rhoda, who has finally convinced me that men are everywhere. She would always say, "When one man leaves there is always another, doesn't matter if you are eighteen or eighty."

To my grandmother Alex, known as Poppy to me, and my stepfather, Mel, who taught me that there are good men out there.

To my sister, Tracey; my brother-in-law, Matt; and my three nephews, Noah, Owen, and Ryder, who showed me that happy endings do exist.

To my aunt Arlene who taught me at the age of fifteen that a woman should be financially independent.

To my uncle Robert who taught me that smart men date and marry older women.

To my friend and writing partner, Lisa Johnson Mandell—I couldn't have written this book without you—and to her husband, Jim. Together they showed me that you can get married after forty and it's worth the wait.

To my spiritual godmother, Dr. Louise Leguina, who is watching over me in heaven. She taught me to "let the wind dance between you when you are in a relationship."

To my staff: Destin, my dearest friend and producing partner, and Rachel, without you holding down the fort I would never have been able to write this book—I love you and wish you true love and happiness. Kisses to Sin.

To my manager, Jeff Federman, for finding me, making me smile, working as fast as I do, and for being my rock in times of chaos.

To my support staff: Allen and David—you don't know this, but fixing my computer, making calls for me, and running errands is what makes my company go round.

Thank you to my agent, Eileen Cope. From the moment I spoke to you, I knew you were the fiercest agent in town, and you did not disappoint. You rock.

Special thanks to the Bravo Network, Rob Lee, and Lance Klein for believing in me.

To my friend Tiffany, who is my hair and makeup artist and gave me the best man-catching power tool of all: long, silky luxurious hair.

To my stylist team of Joanne, Marni, and Allen who taught me that great style starts and ends with a great fit.

To my single friends Rose, Amy, and Sidney—thank you for being so honest and sharing your dating war stories with me.

To Abraham, Esther, and Jerry Hicks who taught me to

manifest my desires, that we are eternal beings who will never ever get it all done, and that the secret to life is not about getting to your destination but that true happiness comes from enjoying the ride to get there.

To the Yoda of courtship, Dr. Pat Allen, who showed me the true way to negotiate monogamy.

Little did I know when I began this book that it would be just as intense as producing a television show, and that I would be lucky enough to work with a "cast and crew" that are the absolute best in the business. My extreme gratitude is extended to Judith Curr, publisher of Atria Books; Amy Tannenbaum, my editor extraordinaire; Kathleen Schmidt, Christine Duplessis, Jeanne Lee, and Isolde Sauer.

There are many female mentors who do not know me but I know them in my heart, and they have made a deep impact on my life. I would like to thank these women for showing me that we can achieve our dreams if we just believe, and pay the price with hard work: Dr. Pat Allen, Suze Orman, Oprah Winfrey, Martha Stewart, Madonna, Hillary Clinton, Marianne Williamson, Judy Blume, Judge Judy, Rhonda Byrne, Suzanne Somers, Candace Bushnell, Dany Levy, J. K. Rowling, Paula Deen, and Sherry Lansing.

May the universe bring us many more women like this.

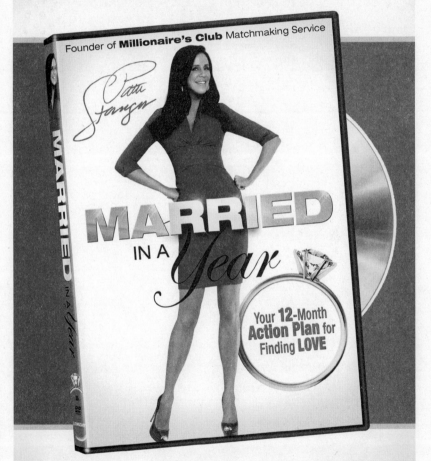